D0675453

Expression
of Appreciation

With heartfelt appreciation, I would like to thank every parent, student and staff member for taking the time to collect and submit their favorite recipes.

I would also like to thank all my committee members for helping me proofread all these fantastic recipes.

Without everyone's help, this book would not have been possible.

Thank You and Enjoy!

Michelle Kennedy

SEASONED WITH LOVE

Sponsored by

LAMPLIGHTER SCHOOL

Memphis, Tennessee

OFFICERS

Organizer..Michelle Kennedy

Advisor..Heidi Nelson

Advisor...Sherry Hulen

PROOFREADERS

Nancy McHugh
Jan Morrell
Donna Summers

DEDICATION

We dedicate this book to all of our Lamplighter families whose family lives are as always centered around the kitchen.

Some of the recipes are treasured family keepsakes, favorites from childhood, and some are invented by those who love to create something special for their families as a love offering.

Our thanks to all who generously contributed their favorite recipes. Without the help of Lamplighter families and the Lamplighter Cookbook Committee who envisioned, encouraged and formatted this wonderful collection for all of us to enjoy, this work simply could not have been accomplished.

We hope you will enjoy the outstanding, treasured recipes which follow and have fun looking for special recipes from Lamplighter friends.

LAMPLIGHTER MONTESSORI SCHOOL

An affiliate of the American Montessori Society
and a Tennessee state approved school.
The school has four locations serving toddlers,
pre-school ages and elementary children at:

751 N. Trezevant
Memphis, TN 38112
901/323-2128

1021 Mosby Road
Memphis, TN 38116
901/332-7500

8512 Farmington Blvd.
Germantown, TN 38138
901/753-5437

6865 Poplar Pike
Memphis, TN 38119
901/757-4093

MEMPHIS MONTESSORI INSTITUTE

A fully accredited American Montessori Society Teacher
Preparation Program to prepare adults to teach
3 to 5-year-old children is housed at LMS and nationally certifies
Montessori teachers.

1021 Mosby Road
Memphis, TN 38116
901/332-7500

Vinca Minor
Anna, Age 6

Your Favorite Recipes

Recipe   Page Number

FUNDCRAFT PUBLISHING, INC.
Specializing In Fund-raising Cookbooks
410 Highway 72W., P.O. Box 340
Collierville, TN 38017

Appetizers
Relishes & Pickles

# *Appetizers*

Appetizers are those treats that can be served either at the start of a meal or at a reception or open house. Listed below are quick appetizers that can be served anytime with crackers, thin sliced toasted bread or potato chips:

1. Caviar flavored with onion juice.
2. Cream cheese with chopped chutney and dash of curry powder.
3. Lobster tail moistened with lemon juice.
4. Almonds or pecans roasted and chopped, then mixed with anchovy paste.
5. Cream cheese with chopped pickle.
6. Chicken livers minced and moistened with mayonnaise.
7. Cheese squares with olive attached by toothpick.
8. Liverwurst with pistachio nuts.
9. Sardines with caviar paste.
10. Minced eggs with anchovies.
11. Cream cheese and horseradish.
12. Cream cheese and anchovy paste with grated onion.
13. Herring squares mashed in its own juice with dash of vinegar and Tabasco sauce.
14. Peanut butter and bacon toasted on dark bread.
15. Deviled ham with chopped onions and Spanish olives.
16. Stilton cheese moistened with Port wine.
17. Shrimp flavored with French dressing.
18. Caviar mixed with cream cheese with dash of Worcestershire sauce.
19. Peanuts roasted, crushed and mixed with anchovy paste.
20. Sardine slices topped with chopped olives.
21. Pimento cheese mixed with a dash of horseradish.
22. Minced shrimp with onion juice.
23. Cream cheese with dash of Worcestershire sauce and chives.

APPETIZERS, RELISHES & PICKLES

ALOHA SPREAD

8 oz. cream cheese
1 c. crushed pineapple
1 c. flaked coconut

1 1/2 tsp. ginger
2 tsp. lemon juice
1/2 c. chopped pecans

Beat cream cheese in mixer bowl until light and fluffy. Add pineapple, coconut, ginger and lemon juice; mix well. Stir in pecans. Chill until serving time. Serve with bite-sized fresh fruit.

Valerie Speakman

ARTICHOKE DIP

1 can artichoke hearts,
    drained and mashed

1 c. Parmesan cheese
3/4 c. mayonnaise

Mix together and bake for 30 minutes at 350°. Serve with crackers.

Becky Cunningham

ARTICHOKE DIP

1 can artichoke hearts,
    quartered
3 Tbsp. mayonnaise

1 Tbsp. Parmesan cheese
1/2 tsp. garlic salt
1 Tbsp. cooking sherry

Mix all together and bake 10 minutes until hot at 350°.

Vicki Less

HOT ARTICHOKE DIP

1 (4 oz.) jar pimento, diced
1 (14 oz.) can artichoke
    hearts
1 1/2 c. mayonnaise

2 cans diced green chilies,
    drained
4 oz. Monterey Jack cheese,
    shredded
1/2 c. Parmesan cheese

Drain pimentos and reserve 2 teaspoons for top. Drain and chop artichoke hearts. In medium bowl, mix pimento, artichokes, mayonnaise, green chiles, Parmesan cheese and Monterey Jack cheese.

Spoon into 1 1/2 quart baking dish. Sprinkle with

Parmesan and reserved pimento. Bake, uncovered, in 325° oven for 30 minutes. Prepare at least 1 hour before serving.

Lynette Clemmons

BEER CHEESE

12 oz. cold pack Cheddar at
room temperature
1/2 to 3/4 tsp. cayenne
pepper

1/4 to 1/2 tsp. garlic powder
1/4 to 1/2 tsp. onion powder
stale beer to taste

Combine all ingredients except beer. Mix well. Add beer until mixture reaches desired spreading consistency. Chill.

Sherry Hulen

BLEU CHEESE BALL

1 (8 oz.) pkg. cream cheese
5 oz. Bleu cheese
1 tsp. basil
1 tsp. seasoned salt

1 Tbsp. grated onion
1 tsp. Worcestershire sauce
1/2 c. chopped nuts

Combine ingredients into a ball. Roll in finely chopped nuts. Flavor is even better if made a day or two ahead. Freezes well.

Donna Davis

BROCCOLI DIP

1 pkg. frozen chopped
broccoli
1 onion, finely chopped
1 can mushroom soup

1 stick oleo
1 pkg. garlic cheese
1 small can mushrooms,
chopped

Saute onion in oleo. Cook broccoli as directed. Drain well. Add onion and other ingredients, blending thoroughly. Serve in chafing dish with crackers or Melba rounds.

Sherry Hulen

CHEESE BALL

2 pkg. Philly cream cheese,
soft
2 pkg. Mrs. Weaver's thin
beef

1 onion, chopped fine
1 tsp. Accent
2 Tbsp. Worcestershire sauce

Put beef in blender and chop up fine. Then mix all ingredients together and shape into ball. Chill in refrigerator for 1 hour.

Serve with crackers, any kind, but bacon flavor or butter flavor crackers are very good with cheese ball.

Debi Malkiewicz

JUDY'S CHEESE DIP

1 stick butter	1 tsp. paprika
4 Tbsp. flour	2 c. milk
1 1/2 tsp. chili powder	8 to 10 oz. Velveeta
1 1/2 tsp. ground cumin	1 to 2 jalapeno peppers
1/2 tsp. dry mustard	

Melt butter in double boiler. Add spices, flour and milk to make a sauce. Add cheese and chopped peppers. Add extra chili powder and hot pepper as desired.

Serve hot with Fritos.

Nancy White

CHEESY-BEEF SPREAD

8 oz. soft cream cheese	4 Tbsp. mayonnaise
1 jar dried beef, chopped	hot pepper sauce
5 green onions	garlic salt

Rinse and dry chopped, dried beef. Chop green onions. Mix remaining ingredients together thoroughly. Add beef and onions.

May be served chilled or at room temperature. Serve with Melba toast rounds.

Michelle Kennedy

CHIPPED BEEF SPREAD

1 (6 oz.) pkg. dried, chipped beef	1 Tbsp. fresh green onion, finely chopped or 1/2 Tbsp. dried green onion
1 (8 oz.) pkg. cream cheese, softened	dried parsley to taste (start with 1 tsp.)
3 Tbsp. mayonnaise	dash of garlic salt
1 1/2 tsp. Worcestershire sauce	

Rinse chipped beef in water to remove excess salt. Then pat dry with paper towels. Cut beef into pieces. Cream softened cream cheese well, then mix in mayonnaise. Add spices, then add chipped beef.

Note: Mix by hand, not with a mixer or blender. Thus spake my mother-in-law, and since this is her recipe, I heed her words. Also, I think this stuff tastes best on Triscuit or rye crackers.

Bebe Schroer

CRABMEAT DIP

1 (8 oz.) pkg. cream cheese
1 (12 oz.) bottle seafood
  sauce

1 small can crabmeat
1 box Triscuits
parsley (for garnishing)

On serving plate, spread layer of cream cheese. Pour on seafood sauce and spread evenly. Crumble crabmeat (drained) over the top.

Garnish with parsley. Serve with Triscuits.

Nancy McHugh

HOT CRAB DIP

1 (3 oz.) pkg. cream cheese,
  softened
1/2 c. mayonnaise
1 (6 oz.) can crabmeat, drained

1/4 c. minced onion
1 Tbsp. lemon juice
1/8 tsp. hot pepper sauce

Beat cream cheese until smooth. Stir in remaining ingredients. Spoon into small ovenproof dish. Bake at 350° for 30 minutes or until hot and bubbly. Makes 1 cup.

Deborah Geels

HOT CHEESE BITS

1/2 c. mayonnaise
1/2 purple onion, chopped
1/2 c. grated Parmesan cheese

dash of salt
dash of Worcestershire sauce

Spread tiny Pepperidge Farm party rolls with butter (thinly). Then spread thickly with mixture and place on cookie sheet. Bake at 325° for 12 to 15 minutes.

Sherry Hulen

FRUIT DIP

8 oz. sour cream
1/4 c. brown sugar

2 tsp. vanilla

Mix together all ingredients and refrigerate at least 6 hours. Serve with fruit for dipping (strawberries, pineapple, etc.).

Olivia Laycook

LAYERED NACHO DIP

1 (16 oz.) can refried beans
1/2 lb. lean ground beef
1 pkg. taco seasoning mix
1 (6 oz.) carton frozen
  avocado (guacamole) dip
1 (8 oz.) carton sour cream
1 (4.5 oz.) can chopped ripe olives

2 large tomatoes, diced
1 small purple onion, chopped
1 (4 oz.) can chopped green
  chiles
1 1/2 c. shredded Monterey
  Jack cheese

Combine refried beans and half (1/2) the taco seasoning mix. Brown ground beef, drain well and combine with remaining taco seasoning mix.

In a 13 x 9 x 2-inch dish, spread beans, then ground beef, then layer remaining ingredients in order. Serve with corn chips.

Note: Sometimes I spoon the nacho mixture onto tortilla chips or tostado shells, then microwave on Low power for a few seconds, just until cheese starts to melt. Yum yum.

Bebe Schroer

MEXICAN DIP

8 oz. cream cheese
8 oz. sour cream
1 pkg. chili seasoning
10 1/2 oz. can bean dip
2 tsp. parsley flakes

5 drops hot sauce
1/4 c. taco sauce
1 1/4 c. Monterey Jack cheese
1 1/4 c. Cheddar cheese

Blend the sour cream and cream cheese until smooth. Add remaining ingredients. Use only 1/2 of each cheese and save the other half to sprinkle on top.

Bake at 325° for 15 minutes or until cheese is melted. Makes a great appetizer!

Leigh Markle

NOW FAMOUS CHEESE RING

16 oz. sharp Cheddar cheese,
  grated and at room
  temperature
1 c. pecans, chopped
3/4 c. Miracle Whip

1 medium onion
sprinkle of garlic powder
1/2 tsp. Tabasco sauce
1 c. strawberry preserves

Do not buy cheese that is already grated. Mix first 6 ingredients together. Shape into ring and chill. Decorate with parsley and put preserves in middle of ring before serving.

Serve on crackers. Good to make up ahead of time (day before).

Sherry Hulen

REAL ONION DIP

2 lb. thinly sliced yellow
  onions
3/4 c. sour cream
4 oz. cream cheese at room temperature

1 tsp. Worcestershire sauce
several drops Tabasco sauce
salt and ground pepper

Place onions in a skillet. Cover and cook over low heat for about 20 minutes. Stir occasionally. Uncover and continue cooking gently for about 45 minutes until soft, sweet and reduced to just a fraction of their original volume. Cool at room temperature, then stir in sour cream, cream cheese, Worcestershire, Tabasco, salt and pepper to taste.

Makes about 2 cups. Good with potato chips or as an omelet filling.

Jan Morrell

ROUND HAWAIIAN BREAD

3 1/2 oz. green chilies,
  chopped
8 oz. medium Cheddar cheese

6 oz. cream cheese
1 Tbsp. Worcestershire sauce
1 round bread

Mix ingredients. Cut out center of bread and fill. Put top back on bread. Wrap in foil and bake 1 1/2 hours at 325°.

Serve with bread pieces or crackers.

Sherry Hulen

SALMON SPREAD

1 (16 oz.) can (2 c.) red
  sockeye salmon, drained
1/2 stick soft butter or
  margarine
1/3 c. mayonnaise
1/4 c. minced green onion
2 Tbsp. dry sherry

2 Tbsp. fresh minced parsley
1 Tbsp. Dijon mustard
1/4 tsp. black pepper
1/4 tsp. minced garlic
1/4 tsp. soy sauce
1/4 tsp. liquid smoke
1 tsp. lemon juice

In a medium bowl, combine all ingredients and chill well. Serve with crackers.

Note: Tastes best with Pepperidge Farm sesame crackers.

Bebe Schroer

SAUSAGE BALLS

3 c. Bisquick
2 c. Cheddar cheese

1 lb. hot sausage
dash of Tabasco

Mix all ingredients together. Roll into balls and mash center down. Bake on cookie sheet at 350° for 15 minutes.

Michelle Kennedy

SHRIMP DIP

2 small cans shrimp, drained
1 (8 oz.) pkg. cream cheese,
  softened
1/2 c. mayonnaise

1/2 small onion, minced
2 Tbsp. lemon juice
dash of paprika

In medium bowl, combine ingredients, mixing well and chill thoroughly. Serve with crackers and chips.

Bebe Schroer

SHRIMP DIP IN BREAD BOWL

2 cans cream of shrimp soup
2 cans cream of mushroom
  soup
2 cans salad shrimp
1/2 c. half and half

8 oz. cream cheese
salt
pepper
red pepper to taste

Mix soup and softened cream cheese. Mix in half and half and spices. Stir until smooth (add more half and half if desired). Add shrimp.

Take loaf of Hawaiian bread. Cut off top and scoop out

inside making a "bowl". Pour in dip. Arrange bread around bowl to dip with. Serve hot.

Better made a day in advance and reheated.

Nancy White

STUFFED MUSHROOMS

1 lb. large mushroom caps
1 medium onion or spring
   onions
2 Tbsp. green pepper, minced
1 tsp. salt

dash of paprika
1 tsp. butter or margarine
3 oz. cream cheese
4 slices bacon, cooked crisp
   and crumbled

Cook onions and peppers in margarine until done. Drain. Whip cream cheese and add rest of ingredients. Spoon into mushroom caps and place in baking pan. Add 1/3 cup water to pan. Bake at 375° for 15 to 20 minutes.

Caution: Cream cheese gets very hot! Cool before serving.

Can put additional bacon, bread crumbs or cheese on top.

Nancy McHugh

STUFFED MUSHROOMS

1/2 lb. fresh mushrooms
1/2 c. fresh bread crumbs
3 Tbsp. crumbled Blue cheese
3 Tbsp. chopped onion

1 Tbsp. minced parsley
1 Tbsp. lemon juice
1/2 tsp. salt

Remove stems. Mince and saute with onion in 1 tablespoon oleo. Add bread crumbs, parsley, cheese, lemon juice and salt; blend. Place filling in cups and place in shallow baking pan. Bake 8 minutes at 450°. Serve hot.

Sherry Hulen

SPINACH ARTICHOKE DIP

2 pkg. Stouffer's creamed
   spinach
1 (8 oz.) Monterey Jack,
   shredded

1 can artichoke hearts,
   chopped
1 can mushrooms
Parmesan cheese

Thaw spinach according to directions on box. Combine with grated cheese, artichokes and mushrooms. Save some

Monterey Jack to sprinkle on top, along with Parmesan cheese, if desired.

Heat in microwave or in oven until cheese melts.

Michele Arata

SPINACH DIP

1 pkg. frozen chopped
  uncooked spinach, well
  drained
1 c. sour cream
1 c. mayonnaise

1 can water chestnuts,
  chopped
1 pkg. Knorr vegetable mix
onion juice (optional)

Mix all ingredients together real good and chill in refrigerator before serving with crackers or chips.

Note: Even squeeze water out of spinach with your hands.

Christi Hardy

SWEET AND SOUR MEATBALLS

4 1/2 lb. ground beef
2 tsp. onion flakes
2 Tbsp. parsley flakes
2 tsp. Accent or m.s.g.

3 (10 oz.) bottles chili
  sauce
3 (8 oz.) jars grape jelly
1/4 c. oil
salt and pepper to taste

Combine meat and seasonings. Form into walnut-sized balls and saute in oil until brown. Drain and add chili sauce and jelly. Simmer slowly, covered, for 1 hour. Serve in chafing dish with toothpicks. Simmering can be done in crock-pot.

This can be made ahead and frozen.

Belinda Fleming

UGLY DIP

1/3 c. vinegar
1 Tbsp. salad oil
salt and pepper to taste
3 tomatoes
1 onion

1 small bell pepper
1 (4 oz.) can chopped green
  chilies, ripe olives and
  mushrooms

Mix vinegar, salad oil, salt and pepper together. Pour over vegetables and marinate overnight.

The Lefors

VEGETABLE NIBBLES

1 zucchini (medium size)
cherry tomatoes

green pepper squares
cucumber (medium size)

Slice zucchini or cucumbers. Thread slices of zucchini or cucumber slices, cherry tomatoes and green pepper squares on wooden skewers. Serve with your favorite flavor of sour cream dip.

Bonnie & Christopher Churchwell

ZESTY DRUMMETTES

2 to 2 1/2 lb. chicken
  drummettes, washed
1/4 c. red hot pepper sauce

2 Tbsp. seasoned salt
1 (8 oz.) bottle reduced
  calorie Italian dressing

Marinate chicken in seasoned salt 15 minutes (more if you have time).

Combine hot sauce and Italian dressing. Place chicken in baking dish. Pour sauce mixture over chicken. Cover with foil.

Bake in 350° oven for approximately 1 hour. Bake, uncovered, for last 5 minutes.

Delores and Gerald Barnes

Soups, Salads & Sauces

Salads

Additions and Garnishes

Slice hard-cooked eggs
Radishes
Chopped green or ripe olives
Nut meats
Pimento
Green pepper
Sardines
Anchovies
Slivered cheeses
Julienned ham
Chicken
Grated carrots
Cubed celery
Onions - pickled, grated or
  pearl onions
Tomatoes, sliced and dipped in
  finely chopped parsley or chives
Capers
Dwarf tomatoes stuffed with
  cottage cheese
Fresh herbs - sprigs or chopped
Mint leaves
Cooked beets, cut into shapes
  or sticks
Lemon slices with pinked edges
  and dipped in chopped parsley
Raw cauliflower

Tips for Tossed Salads

Always handle salad greens
  with care.

Wash well, drain and dry greens
  before storing; chill well
  before using.

To core lettuce, smack head stem
  end down on counter top. Then
  twist the core out.

It is better to tear greens into bite-
  sized pieces to avoid bruising
  with knife.

Don't cut up tomatoes for a tossed
  salad since their juices thin the
  dressing and wilt the greens.
  Use them only for garnishing
  the salad bowl.

Select only firm, hard, green
  cucumbers. The skin should have
  a slight sheen, but if it is highly
  polished, it is probably waxed
  and the skin should be removed.

Use wild greens such as dandelion,
  sorrel or winter cress for a
  different flavor and texture in
  tossed salads.

About Potato Salad

Potato salad is best made from
potatoes cooked in their jackets
and peeled and marinated while
still warm. Small red waxy
potatoes hold their shape when
sliced or diced and do not absorb
an excessive amount of dressing or
become mushy.

Soup Accompaniments

Clear Soups — crisp crackers,
cheese pastry, cheese-spread toast
strips.

Cream Soups — cheese popcorn,
seeded crackers, pretzels, pickles
and olives.

Chowders and Meat Soups —
Melba toast, sour pickles, oyster
crackers, bread sticks, relishes,
toasted garlic bread.

BEEF GUMBO

2 Tbsp. shortening
1 onion, chopped
1/2 bell pepper, chopped
1/2 c. sliced okra
1 (16 oz.) can tomatoes
2 tsp. chili powder or to
   taste

5 drops Tabasco sauce or to
   taste
1 Tbsp. Worcestershire sauce
2 c. stew meat, venison or
   leftover roast
salt to taste
water (if necessary)

Saute chopped onion, bell pepper and fresh okra in shortening 5 minutes. Add tomatoes and juice. Season generously with chili powder, Tabasco and Worcestershire. Cook over low heat 1 1/2 hours.

If using meat that has already been cooked, add after first hour. If using stew meat, add after 30 minutes. Venison cooks the entire 1 1/2 hours.

Serve over hot, fluffy rice.

Sherry Hulen

BEER CHEESE SOUP

1/2 c. butter
1/2 c. flour
4 c. hot chicken broth
1 1/2 c. cream
1 (16 oz.) jar Cheez Whiz

1 (10 oz.) can beer
1 Tbsp. Worcestershire sauce
1/4 c. fresh chives
   (optional)

Melt butter. Blend in flour and cook over low heat until smooth and bubbly. Remove from heat and add hot broth and cream. Stir over low heat until slightly thickened but not boiling. Add Cheez Whiz and stir until melted. Add beer and Worcestershire sauce. Simmer.

Serve with popcorn. Makes 10 (8-ounce) servings.

Jan Morrell

CLAM CHOWDER

1 can clams, rinsed
1 can cream of potato soup
1 can cream of celery soup
1 can Cheddar cheese soup

1 can whole kernel corn
1 (3 oz.) cream cheese
whole milk

Put all ingredients in large microwavable bowl.

Microwave until cheese melts. Add whole milk to consistency desired.

Patty Calvert

CREAM OF CARROT SOUP

1 lb. carrots, peeled and cut into 1/2-inch pieces
2 medium Russet potatoes, peeled and cut in 1/2-inch pieces
1 medium onion, chopped
2 tsp. grated, peeled fresh ginger
3 c. chicken stock, preferably degreased and unsalted
1 tsp. coriander
salt (optional)
juice from one lemon
4 thin lemon slices
2 Tbsp. chopped scallions

Combine first 6 ingredients in pot. Boil, cover and simmer until potatoes and carrots are tender, about 15 to 20 minutes. Remove from heat; cool, covered.

Mix 10 minutes and puree solids in food processor until very smooth. Mix puree and stock in pot; bring to boil; add lemon juice and salt to taste. Serve with lemon slices and scallion garnish.

Kathy Katze

CREAM OF VEGETABLE SOUP

1 1/2 c. sliced carrots
4 c. diced potatoes
1 1/2 c. broccoli or green beans
2 cloves garlic, minced
1 1/2 c. leeks, sliced (white part only)
2 qt. water
4 tsp. salt
salt and pepper to taste
1/2 c. cream or 3/4 c. half and half
1 1/2 Tbsp. margarine or butter

In soup pot, heat carrots, potatoes, broccoli or beans, garlic, leeks and salt. Simmer until vegetables are tender, about 45 minutes.

Puree the vegetables and broth in blender or food processor in small batches; return it to pot. Add salt and pepper to taste. Add cream and butter. Continue simmering (5 to 10 minutes), stirring occasionally, until butter is melted. Do not bring to a boil.

J. Whitson

FROGMORE STEW

3 Tbsp. crab boil	4 fresh ears corn
1 Tbsp. coarse kosher salt	8 new potatoes
1 lb. kielbasa sausage	2 lb. medium shrimp

Simmer crab boil and salt in 4 quarts of water for 15 minutes. Add new potatoes and simmer for 10 minutes. Add corn and kielbasa and simmer for another 8 minutes. Add shrimp and cook until the shells are transparent. Serves 4.

Martha Brahm,
Fascinating Foods

HAMBURGER BEAN POT SOUP

1 c. dried beans (Great Northern)	1/4 c. uncooked rice
1 can tomatoes	1 beef bouillon cube
1 c. diced celery	1/2 lb. ground beef
1 carrot, cubed	salt and pepper

Wash and sort beans. Add to 3 quarts water and boil 2 minutes. Remove from heat and soak 1 hour. Simmer beans 20 minutes, then add tomatoes, celery, carrot, rice and bouillon.

Brown ground beef; drain and add to soup. Bring to boil. Simmer, covered, for 1 hour. Season to taste with salt and pepper. Ingredients can be doubled.

Vicki Less

LENTEN PEA SOUP

1 lb. (about 2 c.) dried split peas, rinsed	1/8 tsp. white or black pepper
2 qt. water	dash of cayenne pepper
1 bay leaf	3 c. chopped celery
2 cloves garlic	1 c. chopped carrots
1/4 tsp. thyme	1 small minced onion
1/2 tsp. marjoram	2 tsp. ground cumin (optional)
1 tsp. salt	1/2 tsp. coriander (optional)

Place first 9 ingredients in large pot; cover. Bring to boil and simmer for 1 hour. Add vegetables and optional spices, if desired. Cover and simmer 20 minutes. Puree, if desired; season to taste. Soup can be thinned with milk or yogurt and served with rice.

Kathy Katze

MINNESOTA WILD RICE SOUP

1/2 lb. fried bacon or 2
   Tbsp. real bacon bits
1/2 onion or 1 tsp. minced
   onion
1 c. wild rice

1 pt. half and half
1 pt. 2% milk
2 cans cream of potato soup
1/2 lb. American cheese

Cook wild rice until popped. Dice and fry bacon and onion. Combine half and half, milk, soup and cheese on medium heat, stirring occasionally. After cheese melts, it will thicken. Add wild rice, bacon and onion and cook until blended.

The Lefors

POTATO CHEESE CHOWDER

1/2 c. potatoes
2 chicken bouillon cubes
2 Tbsp. butter
1/4 c. green peppers, diced
   (optional)
2 Tbsp. flour

1 tsp. salt
1/8 tsp. pepper
2 c. milk
1 1/2 c. grated Cheddar
   cheese

Dice potatoes and cook in 2 cups boiling water until tender. Drain potatoes and reserve 1 1/2 cups liquid. Add bouillon and dissolve.

Melt butter in saucepan and saute peppers. Remove from heat. Stir in flour, salt and pepper. Gradually stir in potato liquid and milk. Bring to a boil and simmer 2 minutes. Remove and add cheese and potatoes. Stir until melted.

Sherry Hulen

SOUP IN ABOUT AN HOUR

1 lb. lean ground beef
5 c. water
1 (14.5 oz.) can
   no-salt-added stewed
   tomatoes
1 (6 oz.) can low-sodium
   cocktail vegetable juice
   (V-8)
1/3 c. barley
1/3 c. dried split peas

1/2 c. chopped onion
1 Tbsp. beef bouillon
   granules
1/4 tsp. black pepper
1/4 tsp. dried basil
1/4 tsp. oregano
1 bay leaf
3/4 c. chopped celery
1/2 c. sliced carrots

Brown ground beef; drain well. In a pot, combine browned ground beef, water and next 10 ingredients. Bring to a boil. Reduce heat. Cover and simmer 30 minutes. Add celery and carrots. Cover and simmer 30 minutes. Remove bay leaf and serve.

Note: I'm an impatient person and frequently just throw all the ingredients in a pot and simmer it for about an hour. This is okay with the other two members of my family who prefer their veggies on the mushy side. What I'm saying here is this: You need not mollycoddle this soup. Also, I like to serve this with corn-oat muffins. Recipe in bread section.

Bebe Schroer

SPINACH CHEESE NOODLE SOUP

2 Tbsp. salad oil
1/2 or 1 c. chopped onion
1 clove garlic, chopped
3 c. water
3 chicken bouillon cubes
4 oz. fine egg noodles
1 Tbsp. salt

3 c. milk
1 (10 oz.) pkg. frozen
   chopped spinach, thawed
   and drained
1/4 lb. shredded Cheddar
   cheese
1/4 lb. shredded Swiss cheese

In large saucepan heat oil. Add chopped onion and crushed garlic. Saute over medium heat until onion is tender (4 to 5 minutes). Add water and bouillon cubes. Heat to rapid boil. Add salt and gradually add noodles so that broth continues to boil. Cook, uncovered, until noodles are tender.

Stir in milk, spinach, Cheddar and Swiss cheeses. Cook until heated through and cheese is melted. Do not boil (stir so cheese doesn't stick.) Sprinkle each serving with paprika and croutons.

Sue Sutherland

TACO SOUP

1 1/2 lb. ground chuck or
   turkey
1 large onion, chopped
28 oz. can tomatoes with
   juice

1 can whole kernel corn,
   undrained
1 (8 oz.) can tomato sauce
1 pkg. taco seasoning
2 cans kidney beans,
   undrained

Brown and drain meat. Mix all ingredients and heat. Serve with chips, sour cream, grated cheese and/or corn muffins.

Gayle Metzger

VEGETABLE BEEF SOUP
(A Half-day Job)

3 lb. cheap cut of beef
  roast, cut into 1-inch
  cubes and trimmed well
1 (1 pt. 2 oz.) can tomato
  juice
1 medium onion, chopped
3 tsp. salt or to taste
2 tsp. Worcestershire sauce
1/4 tsp. chili powder

2 bay leaves
1 (14.5 oz.) can tomatoes
1 c. diced celery
1 small can whole kernel corn
1 c. sliced carrots
2 large diced potatoes
1 (10 oz.) pkg. frozen lima
  beans
about 6 c. water

In a large pot, combine beef, tomato juice, onion, seasonings and 6 cups water. Cover and simmer about 2 hours. Skim excess fat if necessary. Add vegetables. Cover and simmer about 1 1/2 hours longer.

Yields about 8 servings.

Bebe Schroer

WON TON SOUP

6 chicken bouillon cubes
3 or 4 scallions
4 or 5 nappa leaves (Chinese
  cabbage)
12 won ton wraps

2 very thin pork chops
1 1/2 Tbsp. soy sauce
1 tsp. salt
2 tsp. white pepper or black
  if not white

Use large pan, approximately 2 or 2 1/2 quarts.

Melt bouillon in 9 cups of water. Chop scallions and nappa leaves up and add to bouillon and water. Then add soy sauce, salt and pepper. Put all this aside until you have cooked in skillet the pork chops.

Cook chops on low heat in a Pam-sprayed skillet until done. Cut the pork up in small pieces. Add to mixture and cook until won ton wraps are done. Makes 8 servings.

Jeanette Vaughan

ALOHA CHICKEN SALAD

4 c. chopped cooked chicken
2 c. diced celery
1 c. mayonnaise
1 (20 oz.) can pineapple
  chunks

1 c. chopped pecans
2 (11 oz.) cans Mandarin
  oranges, drained
1 lb. seedless grapes

Toss all ingredients together well. Serve on lettuce leaves.

Nancy Fuller McKown

APPLE SALAD

2 large red Delicious apples,
   cored, unpeeled and cut
   into chunks
2/3 c. crushed pineapple,
   drained and juice reserved
   or minced fresh pineapple

1/3 c. celery, diced
2 Tbsp. raisins
3 Tbsp. plain nonfat yogurt
2 tsp. mayonnaise
1 Tbsp. pineapple juice
1/8 tsp. cinnamon

In a medium bowl, combine salad ingredients: apples, pineapple, celery and raisins. In small bowl, combine dressing ingredients: yogurt, mayo, pineapple juice and cinnamon. Pour dressing over salad and mix. Yields 4 (1-cup) servings.

Note: Choose firm, red Delicious apples. I actually prefer Winesap or McIntosh apples if I can get them. If not, I go for Granny Smith, but this salad is good even with red Delicious apples.

Bebe Schroer

BROCCOLI AND CAULIFLOWER SALAD

1 small cauliflower, broken
   into flowerets
1 lb. broccoli, broken into
   flowerets
1/2 lb. fresh mushrooms,
   sliced
2 stalks celery, sliced
1 small purple onion, chopped

1 c. vegetable oil
1/2 c. white wine vinegar
1/2 c. sugar
1 Tbsp. dried Italian
   seasoning
2 tsp. dry mustard
1 tsp. salt
lettuce leaves (optional)

Combine cauliflower, broccoli, mushrooms, onion and celery in large bowl and set aside.

Combine oil and next 5 ingredients in small bowl; stir well and pour over vegetables. Toss gently to coat; cover and chill 3 hours, stirring occasionally.

Serve salad with slotted spoon over lettuce if desired. Yields 8 to 10 servings.

Note: I also trim broccoli stems and slice into small pieces and add to this salad. Also, the amount of oil can be reduced slightly, if desired. Also, I have made this salad the night before, but store the onion in a separate container, then add it to the salad the next day.

Bebe Schroer

BROCCOLI DELIGHT

1 large bunch fresh broccoli	1/2 c. raisins
1 lb. bacon, cooked and	1 c. whole cashews
crumbled	1 c. mayonnaise
1 medium purple onion,	1/2 c. sugar
chopped	2 tsp. vinegar

Cut tops of broccoli into bite-size flowerets and trim stems and slice into 1/4-inch circles. Put in large bowl and add crumbled bacon, chopped onion, raisins and cashews. In small bowl, mix mayo, sugar and vinegar and blend well. Toss dressing on salad 1 or 2 hours before serving. Yields 6 to 8 servings.

Note: To start salad the night before, cut broccoli and onion, storing in separate bags or containers. Make dressing and cook bacon. Store. Microwave bacon slightly before using.

Bebe Schroer

CHICKEN SALAD

2 c. cooked chopped chicken	salt and pepper
2 stalks celery, chopped	garlic powder
1/2 c. chopped onion	Mrs. Dash
1/4 c. mayonnaise	

Mix chicken, celery, onion and mayonnaise together thoroughly. Add remaining seasonings to taste.

Michelle Kennedy

COMPANY SALAD

Salad:

1 bunch red or green leaf	8 to 10 mushrooms, sliced
lettuce	cherry tomatoes
1 yellow bell pepper, cut up	freshly grated Parmesan
1 ripe avocado, cut up	cheese

Dressing:

1/3 c. balsamic vinegar	2/3 c. olive oil

If lettuce needs freshening, soak in a large bowl of ice water. Gently tear lettuce into bite-sized pieces. Spin to dry in a salad spinner or pat dry with paper towels. Toss all salad ingredients together.

Make Dressing: Combine in a shaker cup. Shake well. Pour over salad immediately before serving.

Gail Rodriguez

CRAB PASTA SALAD

1 can crabmeat
1 (8 oz.) pkg. shell pasta

1 (8 oz.) bottle Hidden
    Valley Ranch dressing
Tabasco

Cook shells according to package directions and drain. Place in large bowl and mix with Ranch dressing. Add Tabasco to taste. Drain crabmeat and add to pasta mixture. Serve immediately.

Michelle Kennedy

DIFFERENT TUNA SALAD

1 (6 1/2 oz.) can tuna in
    water, drained
1/3 c. nonfat yogurt
1 Tbsp. Dijon mustard

2 Tbsp. celery, finely
    chopped
1 Tbsp. minced onion
1/8 tsp. curry

Mix together in no particular order and serve. Yields 1 cup.

Note: Serve with lettuce and tomato as a sandwich or with crackers. Also, this is a spicy concoction. (I'm partial to Pepperidge Farms sesame crackers) or with Wasa crisp bread.

Bebe Schroer

GREEK SALAD

1 white onion, thinly sliced
2 tomatoes, quartered
1 cucumber, sliced thin
1 bunch radishes, sliced thin

1 green pepper, sliced thin
6 black olives
1 c. crumbled Feta cheese

Dressing:

1/4 tsp. oregano
1/2 c. olive oil
2 Tbsp. vinegar
1 tsp. dry mustard

1/2 tsp. salt
2 Tbsp. chopped parsley
fresh ground pepper

Mix salad ingredients. When ready to serve, add dressing.

Jan Morrell

ISLAND-STYLE GREEK SALAD

4 ripe tomatoes
1 large green pepper
1 large cucumber
1 small red onion
6 oz. Krinos black olives

3/4 to 1 c. cubed Feta cheese
extra virgin olive oil
balsamic or red wine vinegar
salt and pepper to taste

Slice the first four ingredients into bite-size pieces. Toss. Add olives and Feta. Serve oil and vinegar on the side.
Note: Extra good with crusty bread.

Sara Lyras

MANDARIN ORANGE SALAD

1 head lettuce (romaine)
1 (11 oz.) can mandarin
   oranges, drained
1/4 c. salad oil
2 Tbsp. cider vinegar

1 Tbsp. sugar
1 tsp. soy sauce
1 tsp. sesame seed (toasted)
1 small pkg. almonds
   (toasted)

Break lettuce into bite-size pieces. Arrange oranges and almonds on top of lettuce. Add all other ingredients in a jar and shake. Add dressing and toss just before serving.

Sherry Hulen

MEAL-IN-ONE-TUNA-SALAD

2 (6 1/2 oz.) cans tuna in
   water
2 celery stalks
1/2 onion
1 small apple
2 boiled eggs
4 to 6 heaping Tbsp. mayo

1/4 c. dill pickle juice
1 whole dill pickle
4 tomatoes
lettuce leaves
salt
pepper

In a large mixing bowl, chop up celery, onion, apple,

eggs and pickles into small pieces. Drain tuna; add to mix. Add the mayo and pickle juice to mixture. Stir well. Add salt and pepper to taste.

On a regular dinner plate, place lettuce leaves to cover plate. Slice tomatoes and arrange them in a circle on edge of plate, leaving about an inch from edge. Place a large amount of tuna salad in middle of plates in a round shape.

Garnish with a touch of mayo and a cherry on top. There, you will have a pretty and attractive and a nourishing meal of fruit, fish and vegetables. Serves 4.

Jeanette Vaughan

ROAST BEEF SALAD

1 lb. roast beef
1/2 c. green pepper,
   julienned
1/2 c. red pepper, julienned
1/2 c. celery, chopped
1/4 c. onion, chopped

3 Tbsp. curry powder
1/2 c. olive oil
3 Tbsp. red wine vinegar
1 tsp. oregano
1/2 c. asparagus (optional)

Cut cooked roast beef into julienned strips and combine with the red and green peppers, celery and onions. Sprinkle with curry powder.

In separate bowl, combine olive oil, vinegar and oregano. Whisk well and pour over salad. Add salt and pepper to taste. Serves 4.

Martha Brahm,
Fascinating Foods

SOUR CREAM POTATO SALAD

2 lb. new potatoes, skins on
2 hard-cooked eggs, sliced
1 grated carrot
1 bunch scallions, chopped
1/4 c. parsley, chopped
1/2 c. sour cream

1/2 c. mayonnaise
1 tsp. caraway seed
1/4 c. bacon, cooked and
   chopped
salt and pepper to taste

Boil potatoes until tender and slice. Combine all ingredients, except bacon and mix gently. Adjust seasonings, if necessary. Chill thoroughly and garnish with the bacon and parsley before serving. Serves four.

Martha Brahm,
Fascinating Foods

SPAGHETTI SALAD

1 lb. spaghetti
3 qt. water
1 (8 oz.) bottle Italian
   dressing
1 tomato, chopped

1 bell pepper, chopped
1 red onion, chopped
1 bunch scallions, chopped
2 Tbsp. salad seasonings

Options: Add chopped ham, cooked shrimp, crab, cheese or chicken to make a quick one dish meal.

Cook spaghetti in water until tender. Drain and cool. Chop vegetables and mix with cool pasta. Mix all with salad seasoning and dressing and chill.

Add one or more of the optional items for a cool, quick meal in one. Or add other vegetables to create your own flavor!

Fran Sorrell

SPINACH SALAD

1 lb. fresh spinach
1/2 c. sliced green onion
fresh ground pepper
6 slices bacon
2 Tbsp. red wine vinegar

1 Tbsp. lemon juice
1 tsp. sugar
1/2 tsp. salt
1 or 2 hard-boiled eggs,
   chopped

Wash spinach and discard stems. Pat dry. Tear into bowl. Add onions and pepper. Chill.

Slowly fry bacon until crisp. Remove bacon and drain on paper towels. Add vinegar, lemon juice, sugar and salt to bacon drippings and heat thoroughly. Pour over chilled spinach. Add crumbled bacon and chopped eggs. Toss until leaves are coated. Serve immediately.

D. L. Summers

TACO SALAD

1 lb. hamburger
1 small bottle Catalina
   dressing
1 beef bouillon cube
1/2 tsp. pepper
Ranch Style beans
Doritos

lettuce
shredded Cheddar cheese
1 small onion, chopped
olives, sliced
chopped tomatoes
chopped onions

Brown hamburger with chopped onion and smashed bouillon

cube. Drain all fat. Add pepper and Catalina dressing and can of Ranch Style beans.

Crumble Doritos on plate. Add lettuce, shredded Cheddar cheese, olives, chopped tomatoes and chopped onions. Top with meat mixture.

Patty Calvert

TOSSED SALAD

1 large cauliflower
1 large bunch broccoli
1 red onion
1 c. mayo
1/2 c. oil

1/3 c. white vinegar
3/4 c. sugar
1 tsp. prepared mustard
1 jar pimento
salt and pepper

Chop first 3 ingredients fine. Mix dressing (next 7 ingredients). Pour over salad and toss.

Keeva White

CRANBERRY SALAD MOLD

3 c. fresh cranberries,
  rinsed and drained
  (one 12 oz. pkg.)
1 c. water
1 c. sugar
3 envelopes (3 Tbsp.) unflavored gelatin

2 c. orange juice
1 c. diced celery
1 c. shredded carrots
1/2 c. raisins or currants
1 c. chopped peeled apples

In large saucepan, combine cranberries, water and sugar. Bring to a boil. Reduce heat and simmer for 5 minutes. In small bowl, sprinkle gelatin into orange juice to soften it, then add to hot cranberry mixture. Cool the mixture, then refrigerate until syrupy. Fold in celery, carrots, raisins or currants and apples. Pour mixture into oiled 6 cup ring mold. Chill until firm.

To serve, unmold by dipping mold into lukewarm (not hot) water for about 10 seconds. Tap mold to loosen contents and invert onto platter. Yields 8 to 12 servings.

Note: I use a Bundt pan sprayed with cooking spray. Also, this stuff is great with turkey or just with cottage cheese or yogurt.

Bebe Schroer

CRANBERRY SOUR CREAM MOLD

2 (3 oz.) pkg. red gelatin
1 3/4 c. boiling water

1 can jellied cranberry sauce
1 c. sour cream

Dissolve gelatin in boiling water. Chill until slightly thickened. Beat cranberry sauce and sour cream until smooth. Fold into gelatin. Pour into mold and chill until firm. Serves 4 to 6.

Tastes yummy. Easy and pretty at Christmas time.

Sherry Wims

FRUIT SALAD

1 (14 oz.) can chilled Eagle
  Brand milk
1 (21 oz.) can cherry pie
  filling
1 (15 oz.) can crushed
  pineapple, drained

1/2 c. flaked coconut
1 (12 oz.) Cool Whip
1 (11 oz.) Mandarin oranges,
  drained
1 c. mini marshmallows
1 c. chopped nuts

Beat milk until smooth. Fold in remaining ingredients as listed. Stir well to blend and chill.

Joni Sample

JELLO SALAD

1 small pkg. lemon jello
1 (16 oz.) can crushed
  pineapple, drained
1 (8 oz.) pkg. cream cheese

7 oz. Sprite or 7-Up
  (lemon-lime)
1/2 c. finely chopped pecans

Add jello to 1 cup boiling water. Dissolve thoroughly. Put in blender. Add drained pineapple, cream cheese and pecans. Blend until smooth. Pour into jello mold. Add Sprite. Chill overnight.

Nancy McHugh

MAYBELLE'S ORANGE SALAD

1 small box orange Jell-O
2 c. miniature marshmallows
1 c. boiling water
1 small can frozen orange
  juice, thawed
1/2 c. sugar

1 small can crushed
  pineapple, drained
1 small can Mandarin oranges,
  drained
8 oz. cottage cheese
8 oz. Cool Whip

Pour boiling water over Jell-O and marshmallows. Stir

until well-dissolved. Add remaining ingredients. Refrigerate until set.

D. L. Summers

PEACH SALAD

1 (15 oz.) crushed pineapple
1 (6 oz.) box peach jello

1 (9 oz.) frozen Cool Whip
2 c. buttermilk

Combine first two ingredients and bring to a boil. Let cool and combine with Cool Whip and buttermilk. (Use a wire whisk.)

Johnathan Goree

QUICK FRUIT SALAD

1 (29 oz.) can peaches with
  juice
2 small pkg. frozen strawberries

1 small can mandarin oranges
2 to 3 bananas

Thaw frozen strawberries and combine with peaches. Drain mandarin oranges and add to peaches and strawberries. Chill 1 hour. Add sliced bananas when ready to serve.

Nancy McHugh

WATERGATE SALAD

1 (9 oz.) Cool Whip
1 small pkg. instant
  pistachio pudding

1 large can crushed pineapple
  with juice
1 c. chopped pecans
1 c. marshmallows (miniature)

Mix Cool Whip and pistachio; blend well. Combine all other ingredients and stir well. Refrigerate. (Best made the day before.)

Sherry Hulen

ZIPPY CONGEALED SALAD

1 pkg. lime jello
1 pkg. lemon jello
2 Tbsp. chopped pimento
1/2 c. chopped pecans
1 c. mayonnaise

1 c. cottage cheese
1 c. drained crushed
  pineapple
3 Tbsp. horseradish

Dissolve jello in 1 cup hot water. When jello is cool,

mix in the other ingredients. Put into mold or flat pan. Refrigerate until congealed.

Joyce Kennedy

GAIL'S DRESSING FOR CAESAR SALAD

4 eggs	1/2 tsp. garlic powder
3 c. salad oil	1/2 tsp. oregano
1/2 c. white vinegar	juice of 1 lemon
1 tsp. salt	1/2 c. grated Parmesan cheese
1 tsp. white pepper	2 oz. anchovies, minced

Using a mixer or hand beater, whip eggs until light and frothy. Slowly add oil. In a separate bowl, combine remaining ingredients, then add slowly to oil mixture. Makes one quart.

Jeanine Smith

HORSERADISH SAUCE

1 c. sour cream	1/8 tsp. pepper
1/2 tsp. lemon juice	2 Tbsp. horseradish
1/8 tsp. salt	1/4 tsp. Worcestershire sauce

Combine all ingredients and chill.

Sherry Hulen

BUTTERSCOTCH SAUCE

2/3 c. light corn syrup	1/4 c. butter
1 1/4 c. brown sugar, firmly packed	1/4 tsp. salt
	1 (6 oz.) can evaporated milk

Boil mixture of first four ingredients until thickened. Cool. Add milk. Seal in an airtight container and refrigerate.

Serve over ice cream, puddings or cakes. Yields 1 pint.

Sherry Hulen

HOT FUDGE SAUCE

1/2 c. sugar	1/4 c. half and half
1/4 c. cocoa	2 Tbsp. butter
1/2 c. light corn syrup	1/2 tsp. vanilla extract

In saucepan, combine sugar and cocoa. Stir in corn

syrup and half and half. Stir over medium heat until mixture boils. Stir and simmer 3 minutes. Stir in butter and vanilla. Store in airtight container and refrigerate. Yields 1 cup.

Sherry Hulen

<<< Extra Recipes >>>

<<< Extra Recipes >>>

Meats & Main Dishes

Meat Cooking Chart

Roasting	Weight	Minutes Per lb.	Oven Temp.	Internal Temp.
FRESH PORK				
Rib and loin	3 - 7 lbs.	30-40	325	175 F
Leg	5 lbs.	25-30	325	170 F
Picnic shoulder	5 - 10 lbs.	40	325	175 F
Shoulder, butt	3 - 10 lbs.	40 - 50	325	170 F
Boned and rolled				
Shoulder	3 - 6 lbs.	60	325	170 F
BEEF				
Standing ribs · rare	3 - 7 lbs.	25	325	135 F
· medium	3 - 7 lbs.	30	325	165 F
· well done	3 - 7 lbs.	35	325	170 F
For rolled and boned roasts, increase cooking time 5 to 12 minutes.				
LAMB				
Shoulder · well done	4 - 10 lbs.	40	325	190 F
· boned and rolled	3 - 6 lbs.	40	325	182 F
Leg · medium	5 - 10 lbs.	40	325	175 F
· well done	3 - 6 lbs.	40 - 50	325	182 F
Crown · well done	3 - 6 lbs.	40 - 50	325	182 F
SMOKED PORK				
Shoulder and picnic hams	5 lbs.	30 - 40	325	170 F
	8 lbs.	30 - 40	325	175 F
Boneless butt	2 lbs.	40	325	180 F
	4 lbs.	25	325 F	170 F
Ham	12 - 20 lbs.	16 - 18	325 F	170 F
	Under 10 lbs.	20	325	175 F
	Half hams	25	325	170 F
VEAL				
Loin	4 - 6 lbs.	35	325 F	175 F
Leg	5 - 10 lbs.	35	325	175 F
Boneless shoulder	4 - 10 lbs.	45	325 F	175 F
POULTRY				
Chicken	3 - 5 lbs.	40	325 F	170 F
Stuffed	over 5 lbs.	30	325	170 F
Turkey	8 - 10 lbs.	20	325	175 F
	18 - 20 lbs.	14	325	175 F
Duck	5 - 10 lbs.	30	325	175 F

CHICKEN CASSEROLE

4 chicken breasts
1 stalk celery
1 carrot
1 small onion
1 can cream of mushroom soup

1 (8 oz.) pkg. Pepperidge
  Farm stuffing
1 stick margarine
1 can plus 1 c. chicken broth

Boil 4 chicken breasts with celery, carrot and onion for one hour. Take meat off bones and shred and put in dish. Mix mushroom soup with one can chicken broth and pour over chicken in dish.

Take stuffing and mix with butter or margarine. Add 1 cup chicken broth. Place stuffing on top of chicken and soup mixture. Bake at 350° for one hour.

Debi Malkiewicz

CHICKEN BROCCOLI CASSEROLE

3 c. chicken, cooked and cut
  into small pieces
2 pkg. frozen, chopped
  broccoli

1/2 c. mayonnaise
2 cans cream of chicken soup
curry powder
buttered bread crumbs

Sprinkle chicken with juice of one lemon and sprinkle lightly with curry powder. Cook broccoli and drain. Make sauce of cream of chicken soup and mayonnaise.

In 8 x 10-inch casserole, layer chicken, broccoli and sauce. Top with broccoli and sauce. Top with buttered crumbs and bake until bubbly in a 350° oven about 30 minutes.

Kathy Bradfield

CHICKEN IN CHEESE SHELL

Filling:

1 1/2 c. diced chicken
1 c. drained crushed
  pineapple
1 c. chopped nuts
1/2 c. celery

1 c. sour cream
2/3 c. salad dressing
9-inch pastry shell
1/4 c. shredded cheese

Pastry Shell:

1 1/2 c. flour
1/2 tsp. salt
1/2 c. shortening

1/3 c. shredded cheese
4 to 5 Tbsp. cold water

Make cheese pastry and press into an 8 or 9-inch pie pan. Bake at 350° until flaky 8 to 12 minutes. Let cool.

Mix filling ingredients together. Spoon into pastry shell. Sprinkle with 1/4 cup shredded cheese. Chill.

Paula Payne

EASY CHICKEN (OR TURKEY) DIVAN

2 pkg. frozen broccoli,
  cooked and drained
2 c. cooked chicken or
  turkey, chopped
2 c. condensed cream of mushroom soup

1 c. mayonnaise
1 to 1 1/2 lemons, juiced
grated cheese
croutons (if desired)

Prepare the broccoli and chicken (or turkey). Mix mushroom soup (undiluted), mayonnaise and lemon juice to taste. Layer the ingredients in the order given (broccoli, meat, sauce, etc.). Cover with croutons if desired.

Bake in a 325° to 350° oven until hot and bubbly. Grate cheese on top just before serving.

Margaret L. B. Paydar

CHICKEN PILLOWS

2 boneless chicken breasts
1 tsp. garlic
1/4 tsp. or 4 leaves sage
salt and pepper
2 slices ham

2 slices Fontina cheese
4 Tbsp. Marsala wine
1 Tbsp. balsamic vinegar
4 Tbsp. butter
chopped parsley

Lay the slices of ham and cheese on the chicken breasts and season with garlic, sage, salt and pepper. Set aside.

In small saucepan, combine Marsala, butter and vinegar. Simmer 5 minutes or until butter is completely melted.

Place chicken breasts in an ovenproof gratin dish and pour sauce over the chicken. Cover with foil and bake in 350° oven for 25 minutes. Sprinkle with parsley before serving. Serves 2.

Martha Brahm,
Fascinating Foods

CHICKEN POT PIE

2 chicken breasts
3 or 4 c. broth
1/2 c. Pet milk
1/4 c. flour

2 sliced hard-boiled eggs
1 can peas, drained
2 cans biscuits

Boil chicken in salt water (1 teaspoon) and other seasonings. Cut into bite-size pieces. To broth add milk and flour, mixed with water, to form a thick paste. Let simmer until thick. Add eggs, peas and chicken to thickened broth.

Pour mixture into 2 quart casserole and cool. When cool, add biscuits on top and bake at 400° in oven for 15 minutes. Can brown biscuits slightly before putting on top of casserole.

Sherry Hulen

CHICKEN AND SPAGHETTI

2 chickens
2 Tbsp. chili powder
1 c. celery
1 large bell pepper
1 large onion
1 can mushroom soup

1 can tomatoes
1 1/2 pkg. spaghetti
1 lb. Velveeta cheese
salt to taste
black pepper to taste
cayenne pepper to taste

Boil chicken until it comes off the bone. Cook spaghetti until tender. Cook onion, celery and bell pepper in broth until tender. Combine all ingredients. Add salt, black pepper and cayenne pepper to taste.

Bake 1 hour at 350°.

**Nancy White,
Alan Kennedy's Grandmother**

CHICKEN SUPREME

8 chicken breast filets
8 slices bacon
1 (8 oz.) pkg. dried beef, shredded

1 can cream of mushroom soup
1 c. sour cream

Rinse chicken and pat dry. Flatten with meat mallet. Roll as for jelly rolls. Wrap with bacon. Secure with toothpicks. Sprinkle dried beef in crock-pot. Arrange chicken rolls over beef. Top with mixture of soup and sour cream. Cook on low for 12 hours.

Valerie Speakman

GARLIC CHICKEN

3 1/2 lb. chicken, cut up or
   parts (skinless and
   boneless, optional)
3 Tbsp. peanut oil
1 bulb fresh garlic, peeled
   and coarsely chopped

2 small dried hot red peppers
3/4 c. distilled white
   vinegar
1/4 c. soy sauce
3 Tbsp. honey

Heat oil in large, heavy skillet. Brown chicken well on all sides, adding garlic and peppers toward the end. Add remaining ingredients and cook over medium-high heat until chicken is done and sauce is reduced somewhat.

If cooking white and dark, remove white first, about 10 minutes sooner. Watch carefully so sauce doesn't burn or boil away. Serve over brown rice. A green salad completes the meal.

Marty and Susan Hawkins

LEMON-GARLIC CHICKEN

1 chicken, cut up
1 whole head fresh garlic

3/4 c. lemon juice
1 c. water

Mince garlic (yes, the whole head) finely. (Can use food processor or mortar and pestle.) Add lemon juice and water. Set aside. In nonstick Dutch oven over medium-high heat, brown chicken parts quickly on all sides.

(Note: No oil is needed if using a nonstick pan; add 2 tablespoons oil if not.)

Pour lemon-garlic mixture over browned chicken. Cook over low heat for 1 to 2 hours. The longer it cooks, the more tender and flavorful the chicken.

Gail Rodriguez

CHICKEN AND VEGETABLE STIR-FRY

1/4 c. apricot preserves
2 Tbsp. soy sauce
2 tsp. oil (peanut, sesame or
   vegetable)
1 lb. chicken breasts, cut
   into 1-inch pieces

assorted cut-up veggies:
   onion, green beans,
   mushrooms, zucchini,
   celery, peppers (red or
   green), snow peas, carrots
   or any combination

Preheat wok; add 1/2 oil. Stir-fry veggies until crisp, about 4 to 6 minutes. Remove veggies from wok; add remaining oil. Add chicken to hot wok. Stir-fry until cooked clear through. Add sauce made with preserves and soy sauce.

When heated, add veggies and toss. Serve with rice. Serves 4.

Heidi Nelson

NEAPOLITAN CHICKEN

4 lb. boneless chicken
1 medium onion, chopped
4 medium potatoes, cut in
  cubes
1 large green pepper, cut in
  strips

1/4 c. chopped parsley
1 clove garlic, minced
1 tsp. salt
1/4 tsp. pepper
1/2 tsp. basil
1 lb. jar spaghetti sauce

Combine all ingredients in a crock-pot. Cook on low 6 to 8 hours or on high 3 to 4 hours. Yields 6 to 8 servings.

Teddy Hubbs

TURKEY SLOPPY JOES

1 to 1 1/2 lb. ground turkey
1/2 c. chopped green pepper
1 c. chopped onion
1 c. catsup
1/4 c. sweet pickle relish

1 1/2 tsp. chili powder
1 tsp. Worcestershire
1/2 tsp. garlic powder
1/4 tsp. celery seed

Saute turkey, onion and pepper over medium heat until turkey is no longer pink. Add the rest of the ingredients and bring to a boil. Reduce heat, cover and simmer for 30 minutes. Serve on buns.

Kris Dietrich

BILL'S PORK TENDERLOIN

1 pork tenderloin
1 pkg. frozen spinach
4 tomatoes, peeled and seeded
1/4 c. red wine

1 shallot, chopped
1 clove garlic, chopped
2 sprigs fresh rosemary
2 sprigs fresh thyme

Cook spinach according to package directions and drain thoroughly. Rub tenderloin with fresh herbs and marinate in wine for 20 minutes. Chop tomatoes and simmer with garlic and shallots. Broil tenderloin until done about 30 to 45 minutes depending on size.

To serve: Slice tenderloin into medallions and arrange

in circle on plate. Put spinach in middle of pork and top with tomato mixture.

Bill Kennedy

PORK CHOP SKILLET DINNER

6 loin pork chops
4 sliced potatoes
6 carrots, quartered
1 sliced onion
2/3 c. diced green pepper

2 tsp. salt
1 can condensed tomato soup
1/2 c. water
1/4 tsp. hot sauce

Brown pork chops over high heat in skillet. Cover. Cook over low heat for 15 minutes. Remove chops. Spoon out fat. Starting with potatoes, layer vegetables in skillet and top with pork chops. Sprinkle layers with salt. Combine tomato soup, water and hot sauce. Pour over meat and vegetables.

Cover; cook over medium heat for 45 minutes or until tender.

Vicki Less

PORK CHOPS AND RICE

pork chops (4 or more)
large onion
green pepper
1 1/2 c. rice

1/2 c. parsley
1 1/2 tsp. salt
2 drops Tabasco
2 Tbsp. Worcestershire sauce

Brown pork chops, then set aside. Brown onion and green pepper in same skillet. Add 3 cups hot water. Bring to a boil and then boil for 3 minutes.

Turn heat off. Add rice, parsley, salt, Tabasco and Worcestershire sauce. Place in greased 2 quart casserole dish. Cover tightly. Cook for 1 hour at 350°.

Robin Singleton

OVEN BARBECUED PORK ROAST

1 (7 lb.) pork shoulder
salt and pepper

Worcestershire sauce
1 bottle barbecue sauce

Season pork shoulder with remaining ingredients. Wrap loosely in foil. Place in roasting pan and bake all night on 200°.

Meat will fall off the bone. Chop for sandwiches. Serve with barbecue sauce.

Joyce Kennedy

SMOTHERED PORK CHOPS

6 to 8 center cut chops
1 can cream of mushroom soup

1/2 can water
1 Tbsp. Kitchen Bouquet

Brown chops in skillet. Remove from pan. Add soup, water and Kitchen Bouquet to pan drippings. Stir until smooth. Place chops in casserole and pour in gravy. Cover and cook at 325° for 45 minutes.

Donna Summers

SMOKED SAUSAGE AND RAMEN NOODLES

1 bell pepper, diced
1 onion, diced
4 pkg. shrimp Ramen noodles

2 stalks celery, diced
1/8 tsp. crushed red pepper
1 lb. smoked sausage

Place water in large saucepan. Add smoked sausage, celery, bell pepper and onion. Bring to a boil. Add noodles and seasoning packets. Boil noodles for five minutes and reduce heat. Allow to simmer for 30 minutes. Add crushed red pepper to taste.

Brooke Gladney

CRAB AU GRATIN

3 cans crabmeat
1/4 c. chopped shallots
1/4 c. butter

1 c. light cream
1/4 c. Parmesan cheese
salt and pepper

Cook crab and shallots in butter for 5 minutes. Add cream, salt and pepper. Heat thoroughly. Put into 4 individual ovenproof dishes. Sprinkle with cheese. Put under broiler for 3 to 5 minutes. Makes 4 servings.

Michelle Kennedy

SALMON WITH TOMATOES AND BASIL VINAIGRETTE

1/4 onion, finely diced
1 1/2 Tbsp. red wine vinegar
2 Tbsp. olive oil
2 ripe tomatoes, peeled,
   seeded and diced
2 Tbsp. chopped fresh basil

1 1/2 lb. salmon filet
2 Tbsp. dill
1/3 c. chopped onion
1/3 c. white wine
salt and pepper

Combine 1/4 cup finely diced onion, vinegar, salt, pepper, tomatoes and basil. Mix well. Set aside.

Place the salmon in an ovenproof baking dish. Top with dill, 1/3 cup chopped onions and sprinkle with the wine.

Cover with foil and bake for 15 minutes or until firm. Remove salmon to a platter and top with the tomato vinaigrette mixture. Serves 6.

Martha Brahm,
Fascinating Foods

SHRIMP CASSEROLE

1 (6 oz.) box wild and long
   grain rice
butter
1/2 c. onion
1/4 c. green pepper
1/2 c. sliced mushrooms
1 1/2 Tbsp. flour

1/4 tsp. salt
2 c. canned chicken broth
3 lb. cooked shrimp
1 1/2 Tbsp. Worcestershire
   sauce
Tabasco sauce

Prepare wild and long grain rice. Saute onion, green pepper and sliced mushrooms in 1/4 cup or more of butter.

Prepare cream sauce: In a skillet, melt 1 1/2 tablespoons butter. Add flour and salt, then chicken broth. Cook slowly until bubbly and slightly thickened.

Add vegetables and cream sauce to rice. Stir in Worcestershire sauce and shrimp. Add Tabasco sauce to taste. Bake at 350° until bubbly and thick.

Note: Also good, if you substitute cream of shrimp soup or cream of mushroom soup for the cream sauce.

Jeanine Smith

GREEK STYLE SHRIMP

10 oz. shrimp	juice of 1/2 lemon
flour (for dusting)	1/2 c. white wine
butter	2 Tbsp. Pernod
salt and pepper	4 tomatoes, chopped and
1 onion	drained
1/2 c. mushrooms	4 Tbsp. tomato sauce
1 green onion	1/4 c. Feta cheese
2 cloves garlic, chopped	

Thaw and drain the shrimp. Dust with flour and brown in butter over high heat. Add the salt, pepper, onion, mushrooms and garlic and saute until onion is clear.

Reduce the heat to medium and add the lemon juice, white wine and Pernod. Simmer until the volume of liquid is reduced by 1/2. Add the tomatoes and tomato sauce and simmer for 5 minutes.

Before serving, toss in the green onion and Feta cheese. Serves 2.

Martha Brahm,
Fascinating Foods

SHRIMP SAUTE WITH JULIENNED VEGETABLES

2 sticks unsalted butter	1 lb. peeled medium shrimp
1 c. julienned carrots	1 Tbsp. fresh lemon juice
1 c. julienned onions	1 c. heavy cream
1 c. julienned zucchini	1/2 c. Parmesan cheese
1 c. julienned yellow squash	

In large skillet, melt one stick of the butter over medium heat. Add the carrots and saute for 1 minute. Add onions and saute another minute. Add the zucchini and yellow squash (use only the strips with skin on one side). Turn to high heat and continue cooking for 4 to 5 minutes, stirring occasionally.

Add the shrimp, lemon juice and remaining stick of butter. Cook until butter is about half melted, stirring occasionally. Add the cream; cook until the butter is melted and sauce comes to a boil, about 3 minutes; stir frequently. Add Parmesan cheese and cook until cheese is melted and sauce has thickened. Serves 4.

Martha Brahm,
Fascinating Foods

TUNA CASSEROLE

2 cans tuna
1 can cream of mushroom soup
1 can green peas, drained

1 can water chestnuts,
   drained
1 small can Chinese fried
   noodles

Mix all ingredients except noodles in casserole dish. Top with noodles. Bake at 350° for 30 minutes. Serve over toast or rice.

Donna Summers

LAZY DAISY MEATBALLS

1 lb. ground beef
1 tsp. salt
1/8 tsp. pepper
1/8 tsp. celery salt
1/8 tsp. nutmeg
1/2 c. dry bread crumbs
1/2 c. water

2 Tbsp. grated onion
2 (10 oz.) cream of mushroom
   soup
1/2 soup can water (in each
   can)
1 tsp. Kitchen Bouquet

Mix meat, seasonings, bread crumbs, water and onion. Form into balls (24 small). Roll in flour. Brown in hot fat. (Drain excess grease and add gravy.) Mix soup, water and Kitchen Bouquet. Pour over meatballs.

Cover and simmer 30 minutes. Makes 6 servings. Very good over rice.

Sherry Hulen

COUNTRY STEAK AND POTATOES

1 round steak, tenderized
4 to 6 medium potatoes
1 to 2 medium purple onions
salt
pepper

Kitchen Bouquet
1 to 2 Tbsp. flour water
   (start with 1/2 cup, add
   more as needed)

Trim excess fat from steak. Cut into serving-size pieces and brown in skillet. Place in baking dish. Cover with sliced potatoes, then sliced onions. Add flour to pan drippings and stir until browned. Slowly add water, salt, pepper and Kitchen Bouquet. Keep stirring until smooth. Add more water, if needed. Pour over steak and potatoes. Cover with aluminum foil and cook at 350° for 45 minutes.

D. L. Summers

CHILI

1 Tbsp. salad oil
2 lb. ground beef or turkey
1 c. onions
1 (6 oz.) can tomato sauce
1 1/2 tsp. salt

2 (16 oz.) cans red kidney
  beans or pinto beans
1 c. green pepper
2 cloves garlic
2 (16 oz.) cans tomatoes
1/4 c. chili powder

Saute ground beef, then vegetables. Add everything else, except beans. Simmer for one hour. Add beans and simmer 20 to 30 minutes before serving. Serve with corn muffins, sour cream, grated cheese and chopped green onions. Put chili powder on the table for more heat.

Gayle R. Metzger

EMPRESS CHILI
(A.K.A. Cincinnati Chili)

3 lb. lean ground beef
2 large onions, chopped
1 (15 oz.) can tomato sauce
1 (8 oz.) can tomato sauce
1 qt. water (more if needed)
1 1/2 Tbsp. vinegar
3 1/2 Tbsp. chili powder
1 tsp. cinnamon
1/2 tsp. ground red pepper
1 1/2 tsp. salt

1 1/2 tsp. black pepper
2 Tbsp. brown sugar
5 bay leaves
2 tsp. dry red pepper flakes
8 or 10 whole allspice
2 (16 oz.) cans kidney beans,
  undrained
grated Cheddar cheese
  (optional)
sliced green onion (optional)

Saute ground beef and onion. Drain well. In large pot, combine beef and onion mixture with tomato sauce, water, vinegar, chili powder, cinnamon, ground red pepper, salt, black pepper, brown sugar and bay leaves.

In some cheese cloth or tea infuser put the dry, red pepper flakes and whole allspice. Add to pot. Cover and simmer about 3 hours. When 1 hour of cooking time remains, add kidney beans to pot.

Remove bay leaves and tea infuser holding pepper flakes and allspice before serving. Serve over cooked spaghetti pasta and sprinkle grated cheese and green onion over the top.

Bebe Schroer

LASAGNE

2 Tbsp. olive oil
1 minced garlic clove
1 chopped onion
1 lb. ground beef
2 tsp. salt
1/4 tsp. pepper

2 (6 oz.) cans tomato paste
3 c. hot water
1/2 tsp. rosemary leaves
1 lb. lasagne noodles, cooked
1/2 lb. Ricotta cheese
1/2 lb. Mozzarella

Fry onion and garlic until soft, in oil in heavy pan. Add beef, cooking and stirring until crumbly, then add salt, pepper, tomato paste blended with hot water and crumbled rosemary leaves. Simmer, uncovered, for 30 minutes.

In a shallow dish, put thin layer of meat mixture, 1/2 of the lasagne noodles, 1/2 Ricotta and 1/2 Mozzarella. Repeat. Top with remaining meat mixture.

Bake at 350° for 45 minutes to an hour.

Deborah Geels

LASAGNA-MIDWEST STYLE

2 Tbsp. olive oil
1 lb. hamburger
2 cloves crushed garlic
2 (15 oz.) cans tomato sauce
1 (28 oz.) can crushed
  tomatoes
1 (6 oz.) can tomato paste
1 1/2 tsp. salt
1/4 tsp. pepper
1 1/2 tsp. oregano

1/2 tsp. sage
1 1/2 tsp. Italian seasoning
2 bay leaves
3/8 tsp. basil
1 pkg. lasagna noodles
18 to 20 oz. shredded
  Mozzarella
1 lb. Ricotta cheese
Parmesan as needed

Heat in skillet olive oil. Add meat and garlic and brown. Add tomato sauce, tomatoes, tomato paste and all seasonings. Stir occasionally and simmer 2 to 2 1/2 hours. Remove bay leaves.

Boil lasagna noodles 5 to 6 minutes in salted water. Rinse in hot water and drain.

Layer in large rectangular pan: 1. Thin layer of sauce 2. Noodles 3. Sauce 4. Ricotta 5. Mozzarella 6. Sprinkle Parmesan. Repeat steps 2 through 6 with final layer having noodles, sauce, Mozzarella and Parmesan.

Bake at 375° for 20 to 25 minutes.

Connie Luzwick

GROUND BEEF CASSEROLE

1 lb. ground beef	1/2 c. onions, chopped
1 Tbsp. butter	2 (8 oz.) cans tomato sauce
1 green pepper, chopped	1 (8 oz.) cream cheese
1 (8 oz.) pkg. noodles,	1/2 c. sour cream
cooked and drained	8 oz. cottage cheese

Cook beef, green pepper and onions in butter. Add tomato sauce and simmer 20 minutes. Mix cheeses until smooth. Place noodles in casserole dish. Spread with cheese mixture. Top with meat sauce and cook in 350° oven until bubbly, about 30 minutes.

D. L. Summers

MEN'S FAVORITE MEAT CASSEROLE

2 lb. ground beef	1 can tomato soup
1 large onion, chopped	1 (8 oz.) can tomato sauce
1 green pepper, chopped	1 (4 oz.) jar pimentos,
1 (8 oz.) pkg. noodles,	chopped
cooked	1 1/2 tsp. salt
1 (No. 303) can cream-style	1/2 tsp. chili powder
corn	1/8 tsp. pepper
1 can mushrooms	1/8 tsp. dry mustard
1 (No. 303) can ripe pitted	1 c. Cheddar cheese, grated
olives	

Brown beef, onion and green pepper. Add remaining ingredients except cheese. Place in large, flat pan. Sprinkle with cheese. Let set overnight to allow flavors to blend. Bake at 350° for 45 minutes. Yields 15 servings.

Johnathan Goree

GOOD AND EASY MEAT LOAF

2 lb. ground beef	2 tsp. salt
1 large can evaporated milk	1/2 tsp. pepper
2 Tbsp. Worcestershire sauce	1/2 c. chopped onions
1 c. bread crumbs	1 c. grated cheese (optional)
1/2 c. ketchup	

Mix all ingredients. Place in greased loaf pan. Bake in 350° oven for 1 hour and 15 minutes or until well browned.

D. L. Summers

KRAFT MACARONI AND CHEESE TOSTADA

1 (7 1/4 oz.) pkg. Kraft
  macaroni and cheese dinner
1 lb. ground chuck
1 (15 oz.) can kidney beans,
  drained
1 (8 oz.) bottle Catalina
  dressing

1/2 c. chopped onion
1 Tbsp. chili powder
6 corn tortillas
1 c. sour cream
1 1/2 c. shredded lettuce
1 c. chopped tomato

Prepare dinner as directed on package. Brown meat; drain. Add beans, dressing, onion and chili powder. Cover. Simmer for 10 minutes, stirring occasionally.

Fry each tortilla in 1/4 inch hot oil until crisp and golden, turning once. Drain. For each tostada, first layer lettuce, tortilla, Kraft dinner, meat mixture, sour cream and chopped tomato. Makes 6 generous servings.

Note: Crumbled corn chips or nachos are preferred for the tortillas.

Bettylu Meier,
Grandmother of Alex and
Tori Rodriguez

TALARINA

1 large green pepper, chopped
1 big onion, chopped
4 Tbsp. oil
1 lb. ground beef
1 can tomato sauce
1 can creamed corn

1 can whole kernel corn
1 small pkg. noodles, cooked
salt and pepper to taste
oregano to taste
grated cheese
mushrooms (optional)

Cook pepper and onions until transparent. Add meat and seasonings and cook until meat is well done. Add other ingredients except cheese.

Cook in covered casserole at 350° for 45 minutes. Uncover and cook until thick. Cover with cheese and bake until brown.

Kathy Bradfield

TALERINE

1 lb. ground beef
1 medium onion
1 to 2 c. dry noodles
1 large can stewed tomatoes
1 (16 oz.) can corn Niblets

1 small can sliced mushrooms
1 can black olives, sliced
2 to 3 bay leaves
grated cheese

Chop and brown onions. Add meat and cook until brown but not dry. Add tomatoes with juice. Sprinkle noodles on top, pressing down into liquid, and cook until tender. (If more liquid is needed, use from other cans.)

Add corn, mushrooms, olives and the juice from these, if needed. (Reserve remaining juice to use if mixture dries during cooking.)

Transfer to a casserole. Add bay leaves and bake at 325° to 350° until hot through and through and cooked down some. Grate cheese on top just before serving.

Margaret L. B. Paydar

VERMICELLI PIE

1 (12 oz.) pkg. vermicelli
1/3 c. margarine
1 1/2 lb. sausage
2 (4.5 oz.) jars sliced
  mushrooms
3 Tbsp. finely chopped onions
1 c. sliced salad olives
1 c. grated Parmesan-Romano cheese

2 Tbsp. parsley flakes
1/4 tsp. black pepper
1/2 c. Italian bread crumbs,
  divided
3 eggs, well beaten
2 c. shredded Mozzarella
  cheese

Break vermicelli in half. Cook 15 to 20 minutes in boiling, salted water (until done). Drain well and toss with margarine; set aside. Saute sausage, onions, mushrooms and olives. Add Parmesan-Romano cheese, parsley flakes and pepper. Add this mixture to vermicelli, mixing well.

Butter a 9-inch spring-form pan and sprinkle 1/2 of bread crumbs. Pour 1/2 of vermicelli mixture into pan. Top with eggs and Mozzarella cheese. Add balance of vermicelli mixture and top with remaining bread crumbs. Sprinkle generously with Parmesan-Romano cheese.

Cover with foil and bake at 350° for 40 minutes. Serve with Parmesan-Romano Cheese Sauce as follows.

Sauce:

1/3 c. melted margarine
1/4 c. flour
2 c. milk

1/2 c. Parmesan-Romano cheese
1 Tbsp. parsley flakes

Stir flour into melted margarine. Cook over low heat until bubbly, stirring constantly. Add remaining ingredients and cook until right consistency for sauce. Yields 2 cups. Serves 8 to 10.

M. Cathay Fleming

PATTY'S CHEESE CASSEROLE

1 large curd cottage cheese
(medium size)
1/2 box large Velveeta
(1 lb.)

1 (12 oz.) sharp shredded
Cheddar
1/2 stick butter
4 beaten eggs
1 Tbsp. flour

Put all chopped cheeses in large bowl. Add eggs, butter and flour; mix.

Cook at 350° for about 30 minutes in 1 quart casserole until it begins to bubble and brown. Mixture will be wet but not too soupy. Let set for 5 minutes before serving.

Patty Calvert

DO-AHEAD BRUNCH EGGS
(6 to 8 Servings)

4 Tbsp. butter
3 Tbsp. flour
3/4 tsp. salt
1 1/2 c. Carnation milk
1/2 c. water
6 oz. shredded Cheddar cheese

1 c. sliced mushrooms
1/4 c. chopped onion
12 beaten eggs
1 c. buttered fresh bread
crumbs

Melt 2 tablespoons butter in saucepan. Blend in flour and salt. Gradually add milk and water. Cook over medium heat, stirring constantly, until it comes to a full boil and thickens. Remove from heat. Add cheese and stir until melted. Cover and set aside.

Melt remaining butter in skillet. Saute mushrooms and onions until all liquid has evaporated. Add eggs and continue cooking and stirring until mixture is just set. Fold eggs into cheese sauce.

Pour into a 12 x 7 1/2-inch pan. Sprinkle crumbs over top. Cover and refrigerate overnight. Bake, uncovered, at 350° for 10 minutes or so, until heated through.

Connie Luzwick

SPINACH QUICHE

1 1/2 c. Swiss cheese
1 1/2 c. Cheddar cheese
3 eggs
6 bacon strips, cooked
1 small onion
1/2 stick butter

1/4 c. milk
dash of salt and pepper
1 small pkg. frozen spinach, cooked
1 deep dish pastry pie shell

Beat eggs, milk, salt and pepper. Pour into an unbaked pastry shell. Chop onions finely and put on top of eggs. Place Cheddar cheese on top of eggs and onion. Place spinach next. Place bacon, crumbled, next. Place butter pats next. Place Swiss cheese last.

Bake at 350° for 45 minutes to 1 hour.

Peggy Crawford

SAUSAGE QUICHE

(Serves 6)

10-inch deep dish pastry shell (frozen)
1 lb. sausage
1 lb. fresh mushrooms

6 oz. baby Swiss cheese
1 c. half and half
4 eggs
1/4 tsp. salt

Preheat oven to 350°. Prepare a 10-inch deep dish pastry shell. Bake 8 minutes and set aside. In a large skillet, brown 1 pound sausage, stirring to break into small pieces. Remove sauce from drippings. Add fresh, sliced mushrooms. Cook and stir 5 minutes; drain.

In a large bowl, combine sausage, mushrooms, cubed baby Swiss cheese, half and half, well beaten eggs and salt. Mix well. Turn into prepared pastry shell.

Bake for 45 minutes.

Les Carlew

QUICHE

1 lb. meat (sausage, hamburger or ground turkey)
5 eggs, beaten
2 frozen deep dish pie crusts
1 (4 1/2 oz.) jar sliced mushrooms

1 small onion, chopped
2 c. Mozzarella cheese, shredded
4 c. shredded Cheddar cheese
2 Tbsp. flour
1/2 can evaporated milk

Brown meat and onion. Drain fat. Beat eggs. Add milk

and flour. Mix well. Add mushrooms, meat and 1/2 cup of each kind of cheese. Mix together.

Pour mixture into the two pie crusts. Spread rest of cheese on top. Bake at 350° for about 30 minutes.

The Gladneys

QUICK SPAGHETTI

spaghetti	Italian seasoning
tomato paste	hot dogs
salt	whole kernel corn
pepper	shredded cheese

Cook spaghetti to desired tenderness. Drain. Turn down heat and add tomato paste and water to taste. Add salt, pepper and Italian seasoning and let simmer ten minutes. Chop hot dogs and drain corn. Add hot dogs and corn. Let simmer about 15 minutes.

Garnish with shredded cheese. Make as little or as much as you want.

Bobby Bradley, Sr.

CUBAN BLACK BEANS

2 c. water	6 oz. black beans (about 1 c.), rinsed well in colander with cold water

Group A:

3/4 tsp. crushed dried oregano leaves	3/4 tsp. cumin
1 bay leaf	1/2 tsp. salt

Group B:

2 Tbsp. olive oil	1 chopped carrot
1 red or green pepper	1 stalk celery, chopped
1 small onion, sliced	3/4 tsp. ground coriander
2 cloves garlic, finely chopped	

Group C:

1/4 c. orange juice	juice of 1/2 lemon
1 Tbsp. sherry (optional)	lime juice
1/8 tsp. black pepper	sour cream or yogurt
1/8 tsp. cayenne pepper	

Heat water and beans to boiling in covered, 3 quart

saucepan. Boil 2 minutes. Remove from heat and let stand 1 hour.

Mix in spices from Group A. Bring to a boil and simmer for 1 1/2 to 2 hours.

Saute seasonings from Group B until onion is tender. Add to beans. Cover and continue simmering.

Add Group C to soup. Cover and simmer 10 minutes. Adjust seasoning to taste and serve over rice, sprinkling with lime juice and topped with sour cream or yogurt.

Kathy Katze

TATER TOT CASSEROLE

1 lb. ground beef
1/4 c. onion
1 c. grated sharp Cheddar
    cheese

1 can cream of mushroom soup
1 pkg. frozen Tater Tots
salt and pepper

Mix ground beef and seasonings and brown. Pour off excess fat. Press in bottom of casserole dish. Add layer of grated cheese and layer of soup. Top with Tater Tots.

Bake at 350° for 45 minutes.

Joni Sample

MACARONI AND CHEESE

water

macaroni and cheese dinner

Put warm water in a pot. Pour the macaroni and cheese in pot. Let it cook for a little while. Check and see if it's ready. If ready, pour cheese on the macaroni and cheese.

Kori Bell

HOMEMADE NOODLES

1 1/4 c. eggs
2 Tbsp. salt

3 c. flour

Beat eggs and salt together lightly. Mix in flour (unsifted). Let sit, covered, 20 minutes. Roll out very thin (about 1/4 inch). Cut in squares. Roll each up. Slice. Cook in chicken broth for 20 minutes.

Dawn Brown

AMERICAN CHOP SUEY

1 lb. lean hamburger
1 onion, chopped
1 c. celery
1 can cream of mushroom soup

1 can cream of chicken soup
1 1/2 c. water
1/2 c. raw rice
1/4 c. soy sauce

Brown hamburger, onion and celery. In a baking pan, mix meat mixture with rest of ingredients. Bake, uncovered, 1 hour at 350°. Serve with chow mein noodles.

Donna Funcke

EASY CHICKEN PIE

3 c. diced cooked chicken
1 (10 oz.) pkg. frozen mixed
vegetables
1 can cream of chicken soup
1 c. chicken broth

1/4 tsp. pepper
1 c. self-rising flour
1 c. milk
1/2 c. margarine

Preheat oven to 400°. Grease shallow, 2 quart dish.

Stir together soup, chicken broth and pepper. Let stand. Place chicken and vegetables (frozen) in baking dish. Pour soup mixture on top.

Combine flour, milk and butter. Stir until smooth. Pour over mixture in dish. Bake, uncovered, at 400° for 40 to 45 minutes, or until browned. Let stand 10 minutes.

Donna M. Funcke

TUNA PIE

1 (6 oz.) can tuna
1 c. shredded cheese
1/2 c. green onions
1 c. mayonnaise

1 c. milk
3 eggs
unbaked pie crust

Mix tuna, cheese and onion in one bowl. Place mixture on bottom of pie shell. In another bowl, mix mayo, milk and eggs. Pour over top of tuna mixture.

Bake at 350° for 50 minutes.

Donna Funcke

NANA'S FAVORITE DRESSING

1 recipe yellow cornbread,
  cooked
10 biscuits
6 pieces toasted bread
4 to 5 crackers
1 1/2 c. onion, chopped
2 c. celery, chopped
1 c. celery tops, chopped
1 Tbsp. sage
1 Tbsp. poultry seasoning
2 c. water
1 c. chicken broth
salt and pepper to taste
2 eggs, cooked and diced

Crumble breads into small pieces; set aside.

Combine onion, celery, seasonings, water and broth in large pan. Let boil 10 minutes or until onion and celery are tender. Pour over bread mixture and toss. Add more broth if mixture is not as moist as you like. Cool. Add eggs and mix lightly.

Place dressing in greased baking dish and bake at 300° for 30 minutes.

Sherry Hulen

<<< Extra Recipes >>>

<<< Extra Recipes >>>

Vegetables

How To Can Vegetables

POINTS ON PACKING

Raw pack. Pack cold raw vegetables (except corn, lima beans, and peas) tightly into container and cover with boiling water.

Hot pack. Preheat vegetables in water or steam. Cover with cooking liquid or boiling water. Cooking liquid is recommended for packing most vegetables because it may contain minerals and vitamins dissolved out of the food. Boiling water is recommended when cooking liquid is dark, gritty or strong-flavored, and when there isn't enough cooking liquid.

HOW TO CHECK CANNING JARS

The first step in home canning should take place long before food and equipment are assembled and ready to go. Jars and other supplies should be checked prior to the canning session. In that way, you can replace damaged supplies and purchase new ones to avoid costly delays or inconvenience. Here are some tips to help you.

Choosing mason jars. Jars manufactured especially for home canning generically are called mason jars and must be used when preserving. They are designed with a specially threaded mouth for proper sealing with mason lids. So, can with standard mason jars only.

Preparing glass jars. Check all jars, rings and lids carefully. Discard any with nicks or cracks in top sealing edge and threads that may prevent airtight seals. Rings should be free of dents or rust. Select the size of closures — widemouth or regular — that fits your jar. Wash jars in hot, soapy water and rinse well. Then place in boiling water for 10-15 minutes. Keep jars in hot water until ready to use. Boil lid according to package directions.

Closing glass jars. Always wipe jar rim clean after food product is packed. Place lid on jar with button side up. Screw rings on firmly, but don't force. Do not re-tighten rings after processing or cooling.

A new lid that snaps down and clicks as the jar cools, providing visible proof of sealing, called Magic Button (R) is made by Owens-Illinois. Its red button pops up when the seal is broken. The Magic Mason jars that go with the special lids have metric measurements as well as customary U.S. measurements molded on the side.

Jar transfer. Use jar lifter or long-handled canning tongs to transfer jars to and from canner safely. Place hot jars on rack or towel, allowing 2-inches of air space on all sides for jars to cool evenly.

PROCESSING IN A PRESSURE CANNER

Use a steam-pressure canner for processing all vegetables except tomatoes and pickled vegetables.

Directions. Follow the manufacturer's directions for the canner you are using. Here are a few pointers on use of any steam-pressure canner:

- Put 2 or 3 inches of boiling water in the bottom of the canner; the amount of water to use depends on the size and shape of the canner.
- Set filled glass jars or tin cans on rack in canner so that steam can flow around each container. If two layers of cans or jars are put in, stagger the second layer. Use a rack between layers of glass jars.
- Fasten canner cover securely so that no steam can escape except through vent (petcock or weighted-gage opening).
- Watch until steam pours steadily from vent. Let it escape for 10 minutes or more to drive all air from the canner. Then close petcock or put on weighted gage.
- Let pressure rise to 10 pounds (240 degrees F.) The moment this pressure is reached, start counting processing time. Keep pressure constant by regulating heat under the canner. Do not lower pressure by opening petcock. Keep drafts from blowing on canner.
- When processing time is up, remove canner from heat immediately.

With glass jars, let canner stand until pressure is zero. Never try to rush the cooling by pouring cold water over the canner. When pressure registers zero, wait a minute or two, then slowly open petcock or take off weighted gage. Unfasten cover and tilt the far side up so steam escapes away from you. Take jars from canner.

VEGETABLES

ALABAMA EGGPLANT CASSEROLE

1 to 2 medium to large
  eggplants
salt water
1/4 to 1/2 onion, chopped
1/4 to 1/3 green pepper,
  chopped
2 to 4 Tbsp. butter or
  margarine
1 c. bread crumbs, croutons,
  stuffing or a combination
  of these

1 can cream of mushroom soup
1 to 2 tomatoes, diced
1 egg, beaten
1 c. grated sharp cheese
1/2 tsp. thyme, 1/2 tsp.
  oregano and 1/2 tsp.
  parsley or 1 1/2 tsp.
  Italian seasoning
1/4 to 1/2 tsp. garlic salt
1/4 to 1/2 tsp. Mrs. Dash

Peel and dice eggplant. Soak in salty water for 30 to 45 minutes. Drain well. Boil in fresh water until tender. Drain well. Press out excess water. Saute onion and green pepper in butter.

In casserole dish, place cream of mushroom soup and spices; stir. Add onions, green pepper, tomatoes, bread crumbs, egg and 1/2 of grated cheese. Toss well. Add eggplant and toss again. Top with remaining cheese, a few bread crumbs and paprika.

Bake, uncovered, in a 350° oven until browned and bubbly, usually 35 to 40 minutes. (Can be frozen prior to baking. Can be cooked in microwave.)

Sharon L. Peacock

ASPARAGUS CASSEROLE

1 can asparagus, drained
1 can English peas, drained
1 can cream of celery soup

1 c. shredded cheese
1 can fried onion rings

Layer the ingredients and top with onion rings (or anything crunchy). Bake 15 to 20 minutes in the microwave until everything is bubbly and the cheese is melted.

Joni Sample

BAKED BEANS

2 (16 oz.) Campbell's pork
  and beans
1/2 c. dark brown sugar
4 Tbsp. ketchup

1 c. chopped onion
3 Tbsp. cider vinegar
4 slices bacon, cut up

Mix all together. Bake 1 hour, covered, at 400°. Lower to 200° for next hour (leave covered).

Best if made up day before. If you double recipe, do not double vinegar.

Sherry Hulen

FANCY BAKED BEANS

1 onion
1 lb. ground beef
2 small cans pork and beans
1/4 to 1/2 small bottle ketchup

1/4 c. molasses
1/4 c. vinegar
1 Tbsp. dry mustard

Chop and brown onions. Add ground beef and cook until brown but not dry. Transfer to a casserole dish. Add pork and beans, ketchup, molasses, vinegar and dry mustard.

Bake slowly in a 325° oven until cooked down and flavors are thoroughly blended. Stir occasionally and add molasses if too tart or vinegar if too sweet to suit your taste.

Margaret L. B. Paydar

BOZ'S POTATOES

potatoes (one per person
  makes a lot)
cooking oil
good tasting nutritional
  yeast

recommended seasonings to
  taste: sage, rosemary,
  thyme, pepper, salt, soy
  sauce

In an iron skillet, heat enough oil to cover the bottom of the pan. Quarter the potatoes, lengthwise, and then thinly slice. Add to the oil and add spices that you like. Keep turning the potatoes to keep them coated with oil and to keep them from sticking/burning. Sprinkle a generous amount of "good tasting nutritional yeast" over the potatoes. Turn and coat with more yeast.

Cook about 15 to 20 minutes on medium-low heat, turning until crisp and golden brown.

Boz Beck

BROCCOLI CASSEROLE

1 pkg. frozen chopped
  broccoli
1/2 can cream of mushroom
  soup
3/4 c. sharp Cheddar cheese

1 egg, well beaten
1/2 c. mayonnaise
1 Tbsp. chopped onions
salt and pepper to taste
1/2 c. cheese cracker crumbs

Cook broccoli 5 minutes and drain. Combine other ingredients, except cracker crumbs. Mix with broccoli and pour into ungreased casserole. Sprinkle top with cracker crumbs. Bake for 20 minutes at 400°. (Can be made and refrigerated or frozen before baking. Exclude cracker crumbs until just before baking.)

Becky Cunningham

BROCCOLI-CHEESE CASSEROLE

2 pkg. frozen chopped
  broccoli
1/2 o. butter
1/2 medium onion, chopped
1 clove garlic, minced
1 (8 oz.) can mushroom pieces

2 Tbsp. flour
1 tsp. salt
1 can cream of mushroom soup
6 slices American cheese, cut
  into pieces

Grease a 2 quart casserole dish. Cook and drain broccoli. Saute onion, garlic and mushrooms in butter. Add flour and salt. Stir until bubbly. Add soup; stir. Add cheese and stir until melted. Combine broccoli and sauce. Pour into casserole.

Bake, uncovered, at 350° for 1 hour.

Nancy Fuller McKown

BROCCOLI AND RICE CASSEROLE

1 can cream of mushroom soup
1 pkg. frozen chopped
  broccoli, thawed and
  drained
1 1/2 c. cooked rice

2 Tbsp. butter
1 small onion, chopped
2 c. shredded Cheddar cheese
1/4 c. milk
1/2 c. crushed crackers

Preheat oven to 350°. Melt butter in saucepan. Add onions and saute until tender. Remove from heat. Add rice, soup, milk, broccoli and cheese. Mix thoroughly.

Pour into casserole dish and bake at 350° for 30

minutes. Sprinkle top with crushed crackers and bake an additional 10 to 15 minutes.

Michelle Kennedy

FRIED CORN

3 ears white corn
1/2 stick margarine

1/2 c. milk
pepper

Cut corn off cob. Melt margarine in skillet. Add corn and saute 10 minutes. Add milk and pepper to taste. Simmer 15 to 20 minutes or until corn is tender.

Bill Kennedy

GARLIC CHEESE GRITS

2 c. grits
1 1/2 qt. water
1/2 c. milk
2 rolls garlic cheese

4 beaten eggs plus 1 egg
  white
1/4 lb. butter
salt and pepper

Cook grits in water. Mix milk and cheese with grits. Add well beaten eggs, melted butter and salt and pepper. Place mixture in a buttered casserole dish. Sprinkle with Parmesan cheese and paprika.

Bake at 300° for 30 minutes. Serve piping hot. Serves 6 to 8. Reheats easily. Great to serve for brunch.

Joyce Kennedy

HOME FRIES WITH CARROTS

3 Tbsp. butter or margarine
3 Tbsp. olive oil
2 lb. (4 or 5 medium)
  all-purpose potatoes,
  peeled and thin sliced

1 lb. carrots, peeled and
  sliced
1/2 lb. (2 medium) onions,
  thinly sliced
1/2 tsp. salt

Heat oven to 400°.

In large, nonstick skillet, heat half of butter and oil. Add half of potatoes, carrots and onions. Saute until potatoes are tender-crisp, about 10 minutes. Place in 13 x 9-inch baking pan. Repeat to cook remaining vegetables and place in baking pan. Sprinkle with salt.

Bake vegetables 30 minutes or until crisp and golden brown. Serve immediately.

Sue Sutherland

LIGHT GREEN RICE

1 1/2 c. brown rice
3 c. water
1 (10 oz.) pkg. chopped
  broccoli (still frozen)
1/2 c. to 3/4 c. light
  Cheddar, grated
1/2 c. to 3/4 c. light Mozzarella, grated

1 can cream of mushroom soup
1/2 to 3/4 tsp. dry mustard
1 tsp. Worcestershire
dash of garlic powder
freshly ground pepper to
  taste

Cook rice in water. While rice is cooking, combine other ingredients in a casserole dish and mix well. (A 9 x 15-inch dish works well.) Add rice and mix well.

Bake at 350° for 20 minutes. Serves 10.

Susan Hawkins

MARINATED CARROTS

6 c. carrots, sliced
1 large onion, sliced
1 green pepper, sliced
1 can tomato soup

1 c. sugar
1/2 c. vegetable oil
3/4 c. vinegar
1 tsp. salt and pepper

Cook carrots until tender. Drain and cool. Combine with onion and pepper. Combine soup and remaining ingredients and bring to a boil. Pour over carrots and let stand overnight.

Nancy Fuller McKown

ZIPPY CARROTS

2 Tbsp. butter
1/4 c. brown sugar
2 Tbsp. mustard

1/4 tsp. salt
3 c. sliced cooked carrots
1 Tbsp. parsley

Melt butter. Stir in sugar, mustard and salt. Add carrots and heat, stirring constantly, until glazed. Top with parsley.

D. L. Summers

MEXICAN RICE

1/2 c. chopped green bell
   pepper
1 c. chopped onion
1 clove garlic, minced
1 c. uncooked white rice
2 Tbsp. olive oil
1 (14 1/2 oz.) can tomatoes

1/4 c. water
2 Tbsp. red wine vinegar
salt and pepper to taste
1 c. frozen green peas,
   thawed (optional)
Provolone or Monterey Jack
   cheese, grated (optional)

Saute bell pepper, onion, garlic and rice in olive oil until rice is lightly browned. Finely chop tomatoes. Add tomatoes and juice, water, vinegar, salt and pepper to rice. Cover and cook until rice is done.

Add peas, stirring well. Pour mixture into a 1 1/2 quart baking dish. Top with cheese and bake at 400° until cheese melts. Serves 4 to 6.

Sherry Hulen

PEA PODS AND ALMONDS

1/4 c. chopped green onions
2 Tbsp. butter
1/2 lb. pea pods
1 c. sliced fresh mushrooms
2 tsp. cornstarch

1 tsp. chicken bouillon
   flakes
2 tsp. soy sauce
2 Tbsp. toasted slivered
   almonds

In a 10-inch skillet, cook onions in butter until tender, not brown. Add pea pods and fresh mushrooms. Toss and cook over high heat for one minute. Remove from heat.

Combine cornstarch with 2/3 cup of cold water. Stir cornstarch, chicken bouillon flakes and soy sauce into pea pod mixture. Cook and stir vegetables until mixture thickens and bubbles. Toss with toasted almonds.

Paula Payne

PINEAPPLE CASSEROLE

20 oz. pineapple chunks,
   drained and juice saved
1 c. grated Cheddar cheese
1/2 c. sugar

8 Tbsp. pineapple juice
3 Tbsp. all-purpose flour
1/4 c. butter
1 c. Ritz crackers, crumbled

Mix cheese and pineapple well. Mix juice, sugar and flour. Add to pineapple mixture and pour into quart casserole dish. Combine butter and crumbled crackers and spread on top of casserole.

Bake at 350° for 20 minutes. Serves 6 to 8.
"This is delicious with ham or chicken."

Belinda Fleming

GOLDEN POTATO CASSEROLE

6 medium potatoes
2 c. sour cream
2 c. Cheddar
1/4 c. butter

1/3 c. chopped green onions
1 tsp. salt
1/4 tsp. pepper
2 Tbsp. butter

Boil potatoes until just tender. Peel and grate. Combine remaining ingredients. Spray casserole dish with Pam. Combine all ingredients in dish. Cook at 350° for 20 to 30 minutes.

Gayle R. Metzger

KIM'S POTATO CASSEROLE

3 pkg. cubed hash browns,
  thawed
18 oz. grated Cheddar cheese
2 sticks butter, melted and
  separated

2 c. sour cream
1 can cream of chicken soup
1 onion, diced
salt and pepper
2 c. crushed cornflakes

In greased baking dish, mix together the first seven ingredients. Mix crushed cornflakes with the remaining 1 stick of melted butter. Put on top of potato mixture.

Bake at 350° for one hour. This may be prepared and then frozen before baking.

Michelle Kennedy

POTATO CASSEROLE

2 large baking potatoes,
  diced
1 small onion, chopped
8 oz. sour cream
1 can low-salt cream of chicken soup

1 c. grated Cheddar cheese
salt and pepper to taste
1/4 stick margarine
2 c. crushed cornflakes

Saute onion just until clear and soft. Mix first 6 ingredients together well. Pour into 3 quart casserole, greased. Top with flakes and dot with butter.

Bake at 350° for 1 hour and 15 minutes.

J. Whitson

383391

POTATO CASSEROLE

10 potatoes
Velveeta cheese
1 onion

salt and pepper
bread crumbs

In a casserole dish, spray with Pam. Then slice potatoes and cover bottom of dish. Peel and slice onion. Sprinkle onion slices on top of potatoes, salt and pepper, then slice cheese and cover the potatoes and onions with cheese. Put another layer of potatoes, onions, salt, pepper and cheese until you have a desired amount of thickness.

Bake in microwave for 15 minutes or in oven until done. Then put the last layer of cheese on top of potatoes and crumble bread crumbs on top. Put back in oven until bread crumbs are brown. Serves 6.

Jeanette Vaughan

YELLOW SQUASH CASSEROLE

1/2 c. chopped onion
2 lb. yellow squash, sliced
1 tsp. salt
1/2 stick margarine

1 c. grated Cheddar cheese
8 oz. sour cream
pepper to taste
2 eggs, beaten

Topping:

Parmesan cheese
seasoned bread crumbs

1 1/2 Tbsp. butter
paprika

Steam squash and onion until softened, 8 to 10 minutes. Puree in blender or food processor. Add all other ingredients. Stir on low just until mixed together.

Pour into greased, 2 quart, flat Pyrex dish. Sprinkle on topping; dot with butter. Bake at 350° for 30 to 40 minutes or until middle begins to look puffy.

Serve with smoked pork barbecue and steamed broccoli.

J. Whitson

SQUASH CASSEROLE

1 pt. squash, sliced
1 c. crushed cracker crumbs
1 c. milk
1 c. grated Cheddar cheese

2 Tbsp. butter
2 beaten eggs
salt and pepper

Cook squash briefly. Drain and mix all ingredients.

Pour into greased casserole. Bake at 350° until firm in the middle.

Vicki Less

WINTER SQUASH POTAGE

2 medium-large butternut
  squash
3 onions, sliced
2 large leeks (white part
  only), sliced
1 Tbsp. butter

1 qt. broth
salt and pepper
2 c. milk
grated nutmeg
1/2 c. heavy cream, whipped
1/2 tsp. sage

Prick squash and bake at 400° until they collapse. Cut open, discard seeds and scoop out pulp and mash.

Saute onions and leeks in butter. Cook until soft. Add squash pulp, broth, salt and pepper and cook until flavors blend. Puree in blender. Cool and refrigerate.

Just before serving, reheat soup to boiling point. Add milk and nutmeg. Whip cream with sage and spoon a dollop in center of each serving.

Jan Morrell

SQUASH CASSEROLE

1 egg, slightly beaten
1/2 c. chopped onion, cooked
  with squash
1 can cream of mushroom soup
  or 1 c. milk plus 2 Tbsp.
  flour

1/4 c. butter
1/2 c. cracker crumbs
2 c. cooked squash, steamed
  in steamer 5 minutes
1/2 c. buttered bread crumbs,
  seasoned with pepper

Combine all ingredients except bread crumbs. Place in buttered casserole dish. Top with bread crumbs. Bake in 350° oven until hot and bubbly.

Heidi Nelson

SWEET POTATOES CARAMEL

3 medium sweet potatoes,
  peeled
1 c. sugar
2 eggs, beaten

1 tsp. vanilla
1/2 c. butter or margarine
1/3 c. milk

Caramel Topping:

1 c. brown sugar
1 c. broken pecans
1/3 c. flour

1/3 c. butter or margarine,
   softened

Preheat oven to 325°. Boil potatoes in water until tender; drain. In large bowl of electric mixer, mash potatoes. Add the sugar, eggs, vanilla, butter and milk. Blend until fluffy. Pour into a buttered, 2 quart casserole.

Combine topping ingredients and sprinkle over the potatoes. Bake for 25 to 30 minutes. Serves 6.

Ginny Haight
Tess Carrier

TOMATOES FLORENTINE

2 pkg. frozen chopped spinach
1/2 tsp. garlic salt
1/4 c. mayonnaise

4 to 6 tomatoes, sliced 1/2
   inch thick
Cheddar cheese slices
butter

In shallow baking dish, combine spinach, garlic salt and mayo. Arrange tomatoes over spinach and top with cheese. Dot with butter and bake in 325° oven for 25 minutes. Serves 4 to 6.

The only way my child will each spinach! Quick and easy.

Sherry Wims

ZUCCHINI SUPREME

2 medium zucchini, sliced
1/4 stick margarine
1/2 onion, chopped

2 medium tomatoes, chopped
8 oz. shredded Cheddar cheese
salt and pepper

Melt margarine in large skillet. Saute zucchini and onion until tender. Add tomatoes and cheese. Cook until cheese melts. Salt and pepper to taste.

Michelle Kennedy

Breads, Rolls
& Pastries

Baking Tips

COMMON PROBLEMS
(Common Failures)

CAUSES OF PROBLEMS
(Causes of Failures)

Biscuits

Rough biscuits........................Insufficient mixing
Dry biscuits..........................Baking in too slow an oven and handling too much
Uneven browning...................Cooking in dark surface pan, too high a temperature and rolling the dough too thin

Breads (yeast)

Porous bread.........................Over-rising or cooking at too low a temperature
Crust is dark and blisters
just under the crust.................Under-rising
Bread does not rise.................Over-kneading or using old yeast
Bread is streaked....................Under-kneading and not kneading evenly
Bread bakes unevenly..............Using old, dark pans, too much dough in pan, crowding the oven shelf or cooking at too high a temperature

Cakes

Cracks and uneven surface.........Too much flour, too hot an oven and sometimes from cold oven start
Dry cakes..............................Too much flour, too little shortening too much baking powder or cooking at too low a temperature
Heavy cakes..........................Too much sugar or baking too short a period
Sticky crust...........................Too much sugar
Coarse grained cake.................Too little mixing, too much shortening, too much baking powder, using shortening too soft, and baking at too low a temperature
Fallen cakes..........................Using insufficient flour, under baking, too much sugar, too much shortening or not enough baking powder
Uneven color.........................Cooking at too high a temperature, crowding the shelf (allow at least 2 inches around pans) or using dark pans
Uneven browning....................Not mixing well

Cookies

Uneven browning....................Not using shiny cookie sheet or not allowing at least 2 inches on all sides of cookie sheets in oven
Soggy Cookies.......................Cooling cookies in pans instead of racks
Excessive spreading of cookies......Dropping cookies onto hot cookie sheets; not chilling dough; not baking at correct temperature

Muffins

Coarse texture........................Insufficient stirring and cooking at too low a temperature
Tunnels in muffins, peaks in
center and soggy texture............Over-mixing

Pies

Pastry crumbles......................Over-mixing flour and shortening
Pastry tough..........................Using too much water and over-mixing the dough
Pies do not brown
(fruit or custard)....................Bake at constant temperature (400-425 degrees) in Pyrex or enamel pie pan

BREADS, ROLLS & PASTRIES

BANANA NUT BREAD

1/2 c. vegetable oil
1 c. sugar
2 eggs, beaten
3 bananas
2 c. flour
1 tsp. soda

1/2 tsp. baking powder
1/2 tsp. salt
3 Tbsp. milk
1/2 tsp. vanilla
1/2 c. nuts

Beat together vegetable oil and sugar. Add eggs and bananas, mashed to a pulp. Beat well.

Sift flour, soda, baking powder and salt. Add to first mixture with milk and vanilla. Beat well and stir in nuts.

Bake in a 9 x 5 x 3-inch loaf pan lined on bottom with waxed paper, in moderate oven (350°) about 1 hour. Cool and store airtight.

Carolyn Neal for Patrick

BREAK AWAY BREAD

2 pkg. dry yeast
1 c. warm water
3/4 c. sugar
1 1/2 tsp. salt

1 c. Crisco
1 c. boiling water
2 eggs
6 c. flour

Combine dry yeast in warm water. Set aside.

Mix sugar, salt and Crisco. Add boiling water. When mixture is lukewarm, add yeast mixture. Beat in eggs, mixture and flour. Refrigerate 24 hours.

Roll out and cut with biscuit cutter. Dip in butter. Put in Bundt pan, 3 layers deep. Bake at 350° for 30 to 40 minutes.

Sherry Hulen

BREAKFAST BREAD

1 c. whole wheat flour
1/2 c. all-purpose flour
2 Tbsp. shortening
1/2 c. sugar or honey
1/2 c. pitted prunes, diced

1/4 tsp. cinnamon
1/4 tsp. nutmeg
2 oz. hot water
5 oz. milk
1 tsp. yeast

Put all ingredients in a large bowl in order listed, with yeast sprinkled on top of milk and water. Let sit, covered, for 5 to 7 minutes. Blend. Dough will be sticky. Let rise in warm place, covered, about 45 minutes. Punch down. Put into greased loaf pan. Let rise about 30 minutes, covered.

Bake in preheated 350° oven for 35 to 40 minutes. Let cool completely before slicing. Serve lightly toasted with butter and/or honey and herbal tea. Yields 1 loaf.

I let my dough rise in my microwave oven with a cup of hot water back in the corner.

J. Whitson

TEN-MINUTES TO THE OVEN BRAN MUFFINS

1 1/4 c. All-Bran
1 c. skim milk
1 c. flour
1/4 c. sugar or honey
2 1/2 tsp. baking powder

1/2 tsp. baking soda
1/4 to 1/2 tsp. salt
1 egg
1/4 c. oil
1/2 c. raisins

Preheat oven to 400°.

In a big bowl, mix cereal and milk; let stand for 5 minutes. Mix other dry ingredients. Add eggs and oil to bran mixture, beating it to blend. Fold in raisins.

Distribute batter among 12 greased muffin cups, filling about 2/3 full. Place muffin pan in hot oven and bake for about 20 minutes.

Mrs. Debra D. McClore

BUTTERMILK BISCUITS

2 c. flour (all-purpose)
3 tsp. baking powder
1 tsp. salt
1/4 tsp. soda

3 Tbsp. Crisco shortening
1 1/2 c. buttermilk
10 to 12 pats butter or
    margarine

In a medium-sized bowl, mix dry ingredients and Crisco. Add buttermilk while stirring.

Pour batter on a well floured pastry board. Powder the top with more flour and pat down until it is 3/4 to 1 inch thick. Cut with a biscuit cutter and place on a well-greased pan. Place a slab of butter or margarine on the top of each biscuit.

Bake at 450° until golden brown, approximately 10 to 12 minutes. Makes approximately 10 to 12 biscuits.

Les Carlew

CHEESE MUFFINS

2 c. Bisquick
1 egg, beaten
1 c. milk

1/2 stick margarine, melted
2 c. sharp grated cheese

Melt butter. Add milk and eggs to Bisquick. Add cheese and butter. Stir until moistened. Pour into greased muffin tins, filling about halfway.
Bake 30 minutes at 400°.

Joni Sample

CHOCOLATE CHIP OATMEAL MUFFINS

1 1/2 c. all-purpose flour
1/2 c. quick-cooking rolled
   oats
2 tsp. baking powder
1/2 tsp. baking soda
1/4 tsp. salt
1/2 c. packed light brown
   sugar

1/4 c. butter or margarine,
   melted
3/4 c. milk
1 egg, slightly beaten
1 tsp. vanilla extract
3/4 c. semi-sweet chocolate
   chips or mini chocolate
   chips

Streusel Topping:

1 Tbsp. softened butter or
   margarine
2 Tbsp. flour
1/4 c. packed light brown
   sugar

1/4 tsp. ground cinnamon
2 Tbsp. chopped nuts
2 Tbsp. semi-sweet chocolate
   chips or mini chips

Make streusel topping: In small bowl, combine softened butter or margarine, flour, brown sugar, cinnamon, nuts and chocolate chips. Stir together until crumbly; set aside.

Make muffins: Heat oven to 400°. Grease, line with paper liners or spray with cooking spray 12 muffin cups. In medium bowl, combine flour, oats, baking powder, baking soda and salt. Stir in brown sugar, butter, milk, egg, vanilla and chocolate chips all at once just until moistened. Batter will be lumpy.

Distribute batter evenly between muffin cups. Sprinkle about 1 tablespoon streusel topping onto top of each muffin.

Bake 15 to 20 minutes or until wooden pick, inserted in center comes out clean. Cool on wire rack.

Irresistible warm from oven!

Bebe Schroer

CHOCOLATE, RAISIN, NUT BRAN MUFFINS

1 c. boiling water
2 c. bran flake cereal
1 c. unprocessed wheat bran
1/2 c. plus 1 Tbsp.
  shortening
1 1/2 c. sugar
2 eggs, beaten
2 c. buttermilk

2 1/2 c. whole wheat flour
  (pastry flour if possible)
2 1/2 tsp. baking soda
1 1/2 tsp. salt
1/2 c. chopped pecans
1/2 c. golden raisins
1/4 c. chocolate chips
  (semi-sweet)

Pour water over bran flakes, unprocessed wheat bran and shortening. Mix in the other ingredients as listed. Bake in well-greased or paper-lined muffin tins at 400° for 20 minutes. Batter keeps well, covered, in refrigerator for several weeks.

Kris Dietrich

CORN-OAT MUFFINS

1 1/4 c. nonfat buttermilk
1/2 c. yellow whole-grain
  corn meal
1/2 c. regular oats, uncooked
1/4 c. egg substitute or 3
  egg whites
3 Tbsp. brown sugar or to taste

2 Tbsp. canola oil or other
  vegetable oil
1 c. whole wheat flour
1 tsp. baking powder
1/2 tsp. baking soda
1/4 tsp. salt

Combine first 3 ingredients in a bowl; let stand 1 hour. Add egg substitute or egg whites, brown sugar and oil. Mix well.

Combine flour and next 3 ingredients in a large bowl. Make a well in center of mixture. Add wet ingredients to dry ingredients, stirring just until moistened. Spoon batter into 12 muffin cups coated with cooking spray. Bake at 400° for 20 minutes.

Note: I don't use egg substitute as called for, but have substituted egg whites successfully. Also, I don't like my cornbread sweet, so I only use 1 tablespoon brown sugar.

Bebe Schroer

PAMELA BOSCH'S CORNBREAD

1 c. flour	2 tsp. baking powder
1 c. cornmeal	1/4 tsp. salt
1 c. milk	1/4 c. brown sugar
1 egg	1/4 c. oil

Mix all ingredients and bake at 400° for 20 minutes.

Kathy Katze

JOANNE NELSON'S DILLY BREAD

1 pkg. yeast	2 Tbsp. dill seed
1/4 c. lukewarm water	1 tsp. salt
1 c. creamed cottage cheese	1/4 tsp. soda
(the older, the better)	2 1/4 to 2 1/2 c. flour
2 Tbsp. sugar	1 egg
1 Tbsp. minced onion	soft butter
1 Tbsp. butter	salt

Melt yeast until foamy. Stir in cottage cheese, sugar and onion (softened in butter over low heat or in microwave). Add dill, salt, soda and egg. Stir in flour to make stiff. Set bowl in pan of warm water. Cover with tea towel and let rise 50 to 60 minutes (longer if necessary).

Stir down. Put in greased 1 1/2 to 2 quart casserole. Let rise 30 to 40 minutes (longer if not raised enough). Bake at 350° for 45 minutes. Brush with butter. Sprinkle with salt. Great with soup!

Heidi Nelson

DINNER ROLLS

2 c. warm water	6 1/2 to 7 c. flour
2 pkg. dry yeast	1 egg
1/2 c. sugar	1/4 c. shortening
2 tsp. salt	

Dissolve yeast in warm water. Add sugar, salt and half of the flour. Beat 2 minutes. Add egg and shortening and beat in remainder of flour until smooth. Cover with a damp cloth and place in the refrigerator. Punch down, occasionally.

Next, divide in 1/2, shape ball, cover and let rest 10 minutes. Shape into simple pan rolls. Cover; let rise in warm place until double (30 to 45 minutes). Bake in 400° oven for 10 to 12 minutes. Makes 4 dozen.

Les Carlew

DROP YEAST ROLLS

1 pkg. yeast
2 c. warm water
1/2 c. sugar

1 egg, beaten
4 c. flour (self-rising)
1/2 stick melted butter

Mix together yeast, warm water and sugar. Beat egg and add to yeast mixture. Mix in alternately flour and melted butter. Store in airtight container in refrigerator. (Keeps 2 to 3 weeks.)

Drop in greased miniature muffin tin. Bake at 400° for 15 to 20 minutes.

Sherry Hulen

EASY COFFEE CAKE

1 pkg. frozen Parker House
  rolls
1/2 (3 1/2 oz.) pkg.
  butterscotch pudding mix

1/2 c. brown sugar
1/2 c. nuts
1/2 c. (1 stick) margarine,
  melted

Grease Bundt pan. Put 18 rolls in it. Sprinkle brown sugar over. Pour melted butter over, then sprinkle on the pudding mix, then pecans. Let set on counter overnight (cover with dish towel). Bake 30 minutes at 350°.

Susan Moon Weaver

HIGH-PROTEIN THREE-GRAIN BREAD

2 1/2 c. boiling water
1 c. rolled oats, regular or
  quick
3/4 c. nonfat dry milk
1/2 c. soy flour
1/4 c. wheat germ
1/4 c. packed brown sugar
1/4 c. honey

2 tsp. salt
3 Tbsp. vegetable oil
1/2 c. warm water
2 pkg. active dry yeast
1 tsp. sugar
5 1/2 to 6 c. stone-ground
  whole wheat flour

In very large bowl, combine boiling water, oats, dry milk, soy flour, wheat germ, brown sugar, honey, salt and oil. Cool the mixture to warm. Place 1/2 cup warm water in small bowl; add yeast and 1 teaspoon sugar, stirring to dissolve.

Let the mixture stand for about 10 minutes or until yeast mixture starts to bubble.

Add yeast mixture and 2 1/2 cups of the whole wheat flour to oats mixture. Beat for 2 minutes. Then add enough of remaining flour to form a dough that is easy to handle. Turn dough out onto lightly floured board and knead for about 10 minutes or until smooth and elastic. Put dough in large greased bowl, turning the dough to coat the top.

Cover bowl and let dough rise in warm, draft-free place until doubled in bulk, about 1 1/2 hours. Punch dough down and divide in half. Flatten each half into rectangle 18 inches long and 8 inches wide. Starting from short end, roll up each rectangle, pressing with your fingertips to seal the loaf as you go. Seal the ends and place each loaf in greased loaf pan, about 9 x 5 x 3-inch.

Cover the pans and let the loaves rise until they have doubled in bulk, about 1 hour. Bake in preheated 375° oven for about 35 to 40 minutes or until loaves sound hollow when tapped.

Note: This is a dense, whole grain bread that slices easily and holds together even when thinly sliced.

Bebe Schroer

HOT HUSH PUPPIES

2 1/4 c. Martha White
  self-rising meal
3 Tbsp. Martha White
  self-rising flour

1 Tbsp. finely chopped onion
  (more if desired)
1 c. milk or water
1 c. hot pepper
1 egg

Combine corn meal, flour and onion. Add egg. Gradually beat in milk or water. Drop from a spoon into hot fat where fish was fried. Fry until golden brown.

Mrs. Debra D. McClore

JALAPENO CORNBREAD

1 c. cornmeal mix
1/2 tsp. baking soda
1/2 tsp. salt
1/2 tsp. sugar
3 eggs, beaten
1 c. milk

3 to 4 jalapenos, chopped and
  seeds removed
1/2 c. onion, chopped
1 1/2 c. shredded Cheddar
  cheese
1 tsp. garlic powder

Mix all ingredients together. Pour into a hot greased skillet (iron skillet is best). Bake at 350° for 45 minutes or until golden brown on top.

Lynette Clemmons

LEMON PECAN BREAD

3/4 c. margarine or butter
1 1/2 c. sugar
3 eggs
2 1/4 c. all-purpose flour
1/4 tsp. baking soda

1/4 tsp. salt
3/4 c. buttermilk
1 1/2 tsp. lemon extract
3/4 c. pecans

Bake at 350° for 1 hour and 10 to 15 minutes.

Mix margarine and sugar. Add one egg at a time. Combine flour, soda and salt. Alternate flour and buttermilk, beginning and ending with flour. Add lemon and pecans.

Put in loaf pan and bake. Cool 10 minutes in pan. Remove and cool completely.

Sherry Hulen

MAGIC MARSHMALLOW CRESCENT PUFFS

1/4 c. sugar
1 tsp. cinnamon
16 Kraft jet-puff
  marshmallows
1/4 c. oleo, melted

2 (8 oz.) cans Pillsbury
  refrigerated quick
  crescent rolls
powdered sugar glaze

Combine sugar and cinnamon. Dip marshmallows in melted oleo. Roll in sugar mixture. Wrap in crescent triangle around each, completely covering marshmallow and squeezing edges of dough tightly to seal. Dip in oleo.

Place in muffin tins. Put on foil and bake at 375° for 10 to 15 minutes until golden brown. Immediately remove and drizzle with glaze.

Sherry Hulen

MEXICAN CORN BREAD

1 c. flour (whole wheat or
  unbleached white)
1 c. yellow corn meal
1 egg, lightly beaten
2 Tbsp. honey
3 tsp. baking powder
1/2 tsp. salt

1 c. milk
1/4 c. oil
1/2 c. finely minced onion
2 Tbsp. finely minced
  jalapeno peppers
1 c. corn
1/2 c. grated Cheddar cheese

Heat oil in small skillet. Add onion and saute until onion is translucent. Set aside.

Beat together honey and egg and milk. Combine flour, corn meal, baking powder and salt. Combine milk mixture and flour mixture. Add corn kernels, onions (be sure to scrape all of the oil from pan) and grated cheese. Mix well.

Spread into well buttered, 8-inch square pan. Bake at 375° for 25 to 30 minutes until brown and firm on top.

Mary Burrows

MONKEY BREAD

1 pkg. frozen rolls
1 stick butter

sugar
cinnamon

Melt butter in saucepan. Dip frozen rolls in butter. Layer in greased tube or Bundt pan. As you layer the rolls, sprinkle with sugar and cinnamon. Cover and let rise at least 3 to 4 hours.

Bake at 350° for 20 to 30 minutes or until browned on top and hollow-sounding when tapped on top.

Good for brunch.

Michelle Kennedy

ROSEMARY FOCACCIA

2 1/2 tsp. yeast
1 1/2 tsp. sugar
1 3/4 c. water
4 to 4 1/2 c. flour
1 1/2 tsp. salt

1 Tbsp. olive oil
1 Tbsp. rosemary
1/4 c. chopped onion
1/4 c. chopped onion
1 Tbsp. rosemary

Mix yeast, sugar and water. Let sit 20 minutes. Stir in flour and salt. Coat with oil. Let double in bulk.

Knead in 1 tablespoon rosemary and 1/4 cup chopped onion. Spread on a 9 x 18-inch pan. Top with 1/4 chopped onion and 1 tablespoon rosemary. Let rise 25 minutes in a warm place.

Bake at 350° for 25 minutes or until baked through center.

Martha Brahm

SAUSAGE ROLLS

1 lb. mild or hot sausage

1 batch biscuit mix
(Bisquick)

Mix up biscuit recipe as directed on box. Roll on floured surface. Crumble uncooked sausage on top and roll into 2 long rolls. (Cut down middle between the two rolls.)

Take waxed paper and wrap each roll separately and then wrap in foil. Freeze. Remove and slice desired amount of sausage rolls and cook according to biscuit recipe (usually at 400° for 12 to 15 minutes).

Sherry Hulen

STRAWBERRY BREAD

3 c. flour
2 c. sugar
1 tsp. cinnamon
1 tsp. nutmeg
1 tsp. soda
4 eggs, beaten

1 c. oil
1 c. pecans
1 tsp. vanilla
1 (10 oz.) box frozen
   strawberries, thawed

Mix all dry ingredients and make a well in the center of the mixture. Mix all liquid ingredients, then add to dry ingredients. Gently mix by hand until moistened. Pour into two bread pans that have been buttered and sugared (yes, sugared, not floured!)

Bake at 350° for about one hour and 15 minutes. Makes great gifts.

Jeanine Smith

SUN-DRIED TOMATO AND PROVOLONE BREAD

1:

2 1/4 c. flour
2 tsp. baking powder
1 1/4 tsp. salt
1/2 tsp. baking soda
1 c. grated Provolone
1/2 c. chopped green onion
2 Tbsp. parsley

3/4 tsp. rosemary
3/4 tsp. black pepper
1/3 c. chopped sun-dried
   tomatoes
2 Tbsp. olive oil
2 Tbsp. shortening
2 Tbsp. sugar

2:

2 cloves garlic, chopped
2 large eggs

1 1/4 c. buttermilk
1/3 c. pine nuts

Combine #1 ingredients in a small bowl. Mix #2 ingredients well. Mix #1 with #2. Add buttermilk and pine nuts.

Divide into 3 greased 5 x 3 x 2-inch loaf pans. Bake at 350° for 45 minutes or until skewer comes out clean.

Martha Brahm

SWEET POTATO PIE

2 c. mashed sweet potatoes
1 stick butter
1/4 c. milk
1 1/4 c. sugar

1 beaten egg
1 tsp. vanilla
1 unbaked pie shell

Boil sweet potatoes until tender. Mash, and while warm, add butter, sugar, egg, milk and vanilla. Pour all into unbaked pie shell and bake at 350° until brown.

Connie Newsome

EASY PINEAPPLE PIE

1 (8 oz.) pkg. Cool Whip
1 (6 oz.) can frozen lemonade
1 can sweetened condensed
  milk

1 (15 1/4 oz.) can crushed
  pineapple, drained
1 (9-inch) frozen pie crust

In a large bowl, blend lemonade and condensed milk. Stir in pineapple and Cool Whip. Blend well. Pour into pie crust. Chill in refrigerator for 3 hours or until firm.

Debra and Gerald Barnes

BLACKBERRY COBBLER

5 c. fresh blackberries
3/4 c. sugar
1 Tbsp. cornstarch
1/8 tsp. salt

2 Tbsp. butter or margarine
1 Tbsp. milk
1 Tbsp. sugar
vanilla ice cream

Pastry:

1 c. all-purpose flour
1/2 tsp. salt

1/3 c. shortening
2 Tbsp. cold water

Wash berries thoroughly and drain well. Place in a 9-inch square baking dish. Combine 3/4 cup sugar, cornstarch and salt. Sprinkle mixture over berries. Dot with butter.

Roll pastry out on a lightly floured surface into a 9-inch square. Place over berries, sealing edges to sides of dish. Cut slits in crust. Brush crust with milk and sprinkle with 1 tablespoon sugar.

Bake at 425° for 30 minutes or until crust is golden brown. Serve with vanilla ice cream. Yields 6 servings.

Pastry: Combine flour and salt. Cut in shortening until mixture resembles coarse crumbs. Sprinkle with water and stir with a fork until mixture forms a ball. Yields enough for 1 (9-inch) cobbler.

Johnathan Goree

FRESH PEACH COBBLER

1/4 c. plus 2 Tbsp. butter or
  margarine
2 c. sugar, divided
3/4 c. all-purpose flour

2 tsp. baking powder
dash of salt
3/4 c. milk
2 c. sliced peaches

Melt butter in 2 quart baking dish. Combine 1 cup sugar, flour, baking powder and salt. Add milk and stir until mixed. Pour batter over butter in baking dish, but do not stir. Combine peaches and remaining 1 cup sugar. Spoon over batter. Do not stir.

Bake at 350° for 1 hour. Do not stir. Yields 6 to 8 servings.

Johnathan Goree

AUNT SUE'S CHOCOLATE PIE

2 c. milk, heated
1 1/4 c. sugar
3 heaping Tbsp. cocoa
6 level Tbsp. flour

3/4 c. cold milk
4 beaten egg yolks
1/2 stick butter
1 tsp. vanilla

Meringue:

4 egg whites
1/2 tsp. cream of tartar

4 Tbsp. sugar

Heat the 2 cups milk. Mix sugar, cocoa, flour and cold milk in separate bowl. Add to hot milk. Cook until thick.

Stir in beaten egg yolks, gradually. Cook until thick. Remove from heat. Add butter and vanilla extract. Pour into baked pie shell.

Beat meringue ingredients until peaks form. Top with meringue and brown at 350°.

Debra Beck

BLINI
(Buckwheat Pancakes)

1 1/3 c. white flour	1/2 tsp. salt
1 c. buckwheat flour	2 2/3 c. milk, heated to 105°
4 tsp. yeast	1/2 c. melted butter
1/4 c. sugar	4 eggs, beaten

Combine flour, yeast, sugar and salt. Add milk and butter. Mix gently and add eggs; mix. Let rise 1 hour or until double in bulk. Be sure bowl is large enough.

Cook like pancakes on greased hot griddle. A great treat with smoked salmon or sour cream and caviar.

Martha Brahm

<<< Extra Recipes >>>

<<< Extra Recipes >>>

Cakes
Cookies
& Desserts

Candy Testing

Candy	Degrees	Stage	Cold Water Test
	230-234	Thread	Syrup spins 2-inch thread when dropped from spoon
Fudge, Fondant	234-240	Soft Ball	Candy will roll into soft ball but quickly flattens when removed from water
Divinity, Caramels	244-248	Firm ball	Candy will roll into a firm ball (but not hard ball) which will not lose its shape upon removal from water
Taffy	250-266	Hard ball	Syrup forms hard ball, although it is pliable
Butterscotch	270-290	Light Crack	Candy will form threads in water which will soften when removed from water
Peanut Brittle	300-310	Hard Crack	Candy will form hard, brittle threads in water which will not soften when removed from water
Caramelized Sugar	310-321	Caramelized	Sugar first melts, then becomes a golden brown and forms a hard, brittle ball in cold water

Substitutions

1 c. whole milk
½ c. evaporated milk and ½ c. water ½ c. condensed milk and ½ c. water (reduce sugar in recipe) 4 T. powdered milk and 1 c. water • 4 T. nonfat dry milk plus 2 t. shortening and 1 c. water

1 c. sour milk
1 c. sweet milk and 1 T. lemon juice or vinegar • 1 c. sweet milk mixed with 1 T. lemon juice or 1 T. vinegar or 1 ¾ t. cream of tartar

1 c. sweet milk
1 c. sour milk or buttermilk plus ½ t. baking soda

1 c. sour, heavy cream (for sour milk recipe)
⅓ c. butter and ⅔ c. milk

1 c. sour, thin cream (for sour milk recipe)
3 T. butter and ¾ c. milk

1 c. butter or margarine (for shortening)
⁴/₅ c. bacon fat (clarified), increase liquid in recipe ¼ c. ⅔ c. chicken fat (clarified), increase liquid in recipe ¼ c. • ⁷/₈ c. cottonseed, corn, nut oil (solid or liquid) • ⁷/₈ c. lard and salt • ½ c. suet and salt (increase liquid in recipe ¼ c.)

1 1-oz. square unsweetened chocolate
3 T. cocoa plus ½ T. shortening

1 T. cornstarch (for thickening)
2 T. flour (approx.)

1 T. flour (for thickening)
½ to ⅔ T. cornstarch or 1 T. minute tapioca or 1 whole egg, 2 egg whites or 2 egg yolks

1 c. sifted cake flour
1 c. minus 2 T. sifted all-purpose flour

1 c. sifted all-purpose flour
1 c. plus 2 T. sifted cake flour

1 whole egg
2 egg yolks, plus 1 T. water (in cookies, etc.) or 2 eggs yolks (in custards, etc.)

1 c. molasses • 1 c. honey

1 c. honey
¾ c. sugar plus ¼ c. liquid

1 c. granulated sugar
1 ⅓ c. brown sugar or 1 ½ c. powdered sugar

1 t. baking powder
¼ t. baking soda plus ½ t. cream of tartar

1 lb. cornmeal • 3 cups
1 lb. cornstarch • 3 cups
1 lemon rind • 1 Tbsp. grated
3-4 med. oranges • 1 cup
1 orange rind • 2 Tbsp. grated
23 soda crackers • 1 cup crumbs
15 graham crackers • 1 cup crumbs

CAKES, COOKIES & DESSERTS

APRICOT NECTAR CAKE

Cake:

1 Duncan Hines yellow cake
  mix
1 c. apricot nectar

3/4 c. Crisco oil
4 eggs
1/2 c. sugar

Icing:

2 c. sifted powdered sugar

leftover nectar

Beat cake for 2 minutes. Pour into greased tube pan. Bake at 300° for 1 hour.

Mix powdered sugar and enough remaining apricot nectar to make a thick icing. Ice cake when it is slightly cooled.

Sherry Hulen

CHOCOLATE CAKE

2 c. self-rising flour
2 c. sugar
4 Tbsp. cocoa
1 stick oleo
1/2 c. oil

1 c. water
1/2 c. milk
1 tsp. soda
1 tsp. vanilla
2 eggs, well beaten

Mix together flour, sugar and cocoa. Set aside.

Bring to a boil the oil, oleo and water. Pour over dry mixture. Mix well. Add soda, salt, vanilla, milk and eggs. Beat a little.

Bake in oblong pan that has been greased and floured. Bake at 400° for 25 minutes.

Reeva White

CHOCOLATE CAKE

4 eggs, beaten separately
1 3/4 c. sugar
1 c. flour
1 tsp. baking powder

4 sq. chocolate, melted in
  1 c. milk and cooled
1 tsp. vanilla
marshmallows, cut in half
pecan halves

Beat egg yolks and sugar together. Add chocolate and milk mixture. Then add flour and baking powder, sifted together. Then fold in beaten egg whites and vanilla. Grease and flour a flat pan, 9 x 13 x 2-inch. Pour in the batter and bake in oven at 350° to 375°.

As soon as the cake has been removed from the pan, place the halved marshmallows on it. Ice with Easy Chocolate Icing and put pecan halves on the marshmallows.

Easy Chocolate Icing:

3 sq. chocolate
2 Tbsp. butter or oleo
1 1/2 c. confectioners sugar, sifted
7 Tbsp. evaporated milk

pinch of salt
1 tsp. vanilla
1 1/4 c. confectioners sugar, sifted

Melt chocolate squares and butter or oleo over hot water. Add 1 1/2 cups confectioners sugar, evaporated milk and salt all at once and beat well. Cook over hot water until thickened. Remove from heat.

Add vanilla and remaining confectioners sugar in thirds, beating well after each addition.

Margaret L. B. Paydar

CHOCOLATE STRAWBERRY CAKE

1 box cake mix (dark chocolate or chocolate fudge)
1 lb. confectioners sugar
13 oz. evaporated milk
1/2 c. butter or margarine

1 tsp. vanilla
1 pt. whole strawberries
8 oz. chocolate morsels
8 to 12 oz. nondairy whipped topping

Bake the cake as directed. Use 8 or 9-inch round pans (2 layers). After completely cooled, place a layer of strawberry halves on top. Next place the whipped topping over the fruit. Place the second layer on top and repeat the strawberries and whipped topping.

Sauce: In medium saucepan, place the milk, butter and chocolate over medium heat, stirring often. Once melted, add sugar. Cook for 5 to 8 minutes. Cool and then add vanilla. Serve warm sauce over slices of the cake.

Dr. Gerald Presbury

HEATH BAR DESSERT

1 devil's food cake mix
2 chocolate instant pudding

1 family-size Cool Whip
6 Heath bars

Bake cake in 9 x 13-inch dish. Cut cake in quarters after it has cooled. Make pudding. Crush Heath bars. In a large bowl, layer cake, pudding, Cool Whip and Heath bars. Repeat layers. (Tastes great when made the night before.)

Sue Sutherland

ITALIAN CREAM CAKE

1 c. butter
2 c. sugar
5 eggs
2 c. flour
1 tsp. baking powder

1 c. buttermilk
1 c. coconut
1 c. chopped pecans
1 tsp. vanilla

Frosting:

1 (8 oz.) pkg. cream cheese
1/2 c. butter

1 lb. powdered sugar
1 c. chopped pecans

Butter and flour 3 (9-inch) pans. Cream butter and sugar. Beat in eggs. Blend dry ingredients into butter mixture. Mix in buttermilk, coconut, nuts and vanilla. Bake at 350° for 30 minutes.

Frosting: Beat cream cheese and butter until blended. Add powdered sugar. Spread over layers. Sprinkle with pecans. Refrigerate until frosting sets.

Jan Morrell

LEMON CHIFFON CAKE

2 c. sifted cake flour
1 1/2 c. sugar
1 Tbsp. baking powder
1/2 tsp. salt
1/2 c. vegetable oil
8 separated eggs

2 1/4 Tbsp. lemon juice
1/2 c. water
2 1/2 Tbsp. grated lemon peel
1/2 tsp. cream of tartar
powdered sugar

Preheat oven to 325°. Sift flour, sugar, baking powder and salt into large bowl. Use electric mixer at low speed. Beat in vegetable oil with egg yolks, lemon juice, water and lemon peel.

Combine egg whites and cream of tartar in another large bowl. Using clean, dry beaters, beat until stiff but not dry. Fold 1/4 of egg whites into batter. Gently fold in remaining whites.

Pour cake batter into ungreased tube pan. Tap pan on

counter to release air pockets. Bake cake until springy to touch, about 1 1/4 hours. Cool cake completely.

Run knife around pan sides to loosen cake. Transfer cake to plate. Dust cake with powdered sugar. Top with lemon peel for decoration.

Bitsy Hale

MIRACLE WHIP CAKE

Cake:

2 c. flour
3/4 c. cocoa
1 c. sugar

2 tsp. soda
1 c. Miracle Whip
1 c. boiling water

Icing:

2 c. sugar
1 tsp. flour
1 c. butter

2 tsp. milk
1 tsp. vanilla

Cake: Mix all ingredients. Bake at 350° about 30 to 40 minutes.

Icing: Mix together. Boil until thick. Cool cake and ice.

Nancy White

MY FAVORITE CHEESECAKE

Crust:

1/4 c. butter, melted

1 1/2 c. graham cracker crumbs

Filling:

8 oz. cream cheese
8 oz. plain yogurt
2 eggs

1/2 c. sugar
1/4 tsp. salt
1/2 tsp. fresh lemon juice

Mix graham cracker crumbs and melted butter and pat into pie pan.

Blend cream cheese and yogurt. Add eggs, sugar, salt and lemon juice. Mix well and pour into crust.

Bake at 300° for 45 to 50 minutes. Cool and serve with fresh fruit and whipped cream if desired.

Jan Morrell

OATMEAL HONEY CAKE

1 1/4 c. boiling water
1 1/2 c. quick cooking
  oatmeal
1 stick oleo or butter,
  melted
2 eggs

1 c. honey
1 c. light brown sugar
1 tsp. soda
1/2 tsp. salt
1 tsp. cinnamon
1 1/2 c. flour

Set oven at 350°. Pour boiling water over oatmeal. Let stand 30 minutes. Beat 1/2 minute.

Beat in eggs, melted oleo or butter, honey and sugar. Add sifted cake flour, soda, salt and cinnamon. Bake in a loaf pan for 30 minutes or until done.

Teddy Hubbs

PLUM PUDDING CAKE

2 c. self-rising flour
2 c. sugar
1 tsp. cloves
1 tsp. cinnamon
3 eggs

2 small jars baby plums
1 tsp. vanilla
1 c. Wesson oil
1 c. chopped nuts

Mix all ingredients well, then add nuts. Bake in tube pan at 325° for 50 to 55 minutes.

Cream Cheese Frosting:

8 oz. softened cream cheese
1 lb. box sifted
  confectioners sugar

1/2 stick butter or margarine
1 tsp. vanilla

Cream cheese, butter and vanilla. Add sugar, 1/4 cup at a time. Beat until creamy. Frost cake. Sprinkle with pecans.

M. Cathay Fleming

POUND CAKE

3 c. sugar
2 sticks butter
1/2 c. shortening
4 eggs

3 c. cake flour
1 c. milk
1 tsp. vanilla extract
1 tsp. almond extract

383391

Glaze:

1 c. powdered sugar   lemon juice to taste

Cream butter and shortening. Add sugar. Add eggs. Add milk. Add flour slowly and last, add extracts. (Spray Bundt pan with Pam.)

Put in oven that has not been preheated. Bake at 300° for 1 hour.

Glaze: Mix and dribble over cake while warm.

Peggy Crawford

SOUR CREAM POUND CAKE

1 c. butter   1 small carton sour cream
2 3/4 c. sugar   1/4 tsp. baking soda
3 c. Swans Down cake flour   1 tsp. vanilla
6 eggs   1 tsp. lemon juice

Cream butter and sugar. Add eggs, one at a time, and beat well after each addition. Add half the flour and baking soda. Add sour cream and rest of the flour. Add the vanilla and lemon juice; mix well.

Bake in well-greased and floured tube pan at 325° for 1 1/2 hours.

M. Cathay Fleming

TURTLE CAKE

1 pkg. German chocolate cake   7 oz. sweetened condensed
  mix   milk
1/2 c. margarine   1 c. chopped nuts
10 oz. caramels   1 c. chocolate chips

Mix cake as directed on package. Pour 1/2 batter into greased and floured pan (13 x 9-inch). Bake at 350° for 15 minutes.

Melt margarine and caramels. Mix well. Stir in milk. Sprinkle nuts and chocolate chips over baked cake. Pour caramel mixture over all. Pour remaining cake batter over caramel mixture and bake at 350° for 25 minutes.

Belinda Fleming

APPLESAUCE COOKIES

1 3/4 c. flour	1 Tbsp. Sweet 'N Low (sugar)
1/2 tsp. salt	1 egg
1/2 tsp. nutmeg	1 c. applesauce (dietetic
1 tsp. cinnamon	preferred)
1/2 tsp. cloves (ground)	1/3 c. raisins
1 tsp. baking soda	1 c. All-Bran
1/2 c. butter	

Blend together first 6 dry ingredients in separate bowl. In another bowl, cream butter and add sugar and egg. Mix well. Add flour mixture and applesauce, alternately, mixing well after each addition. Fold in raisins and All-Bran.

Drop by level tablespoons onto greased cookie sheet about 1 inch apart. Bake 20 minutes or until bottoms are golden brown. (Middle will be soft.) Set oven to 375°.

Connie Luzwick

BOILED COOKIES

2 c. sugar	2 Tbsp. peanut butter
1/2 c. milk	1 tsp. vanilla
3 Tbsp. cocoa	2 1/2 c. quick oatmeal
1 stick margarine	

Boil sugar, milk, cocoa and margarine 2 1/2 minutes. Remove from heat. Add peanut butter and vanilla. Add quick oatmeal. Drop on wax paper immediately.

Bitsy Hale

BUCKEYES
(AKA Peanut Butter Balls)

2 sticks margarine	1 (12 oz.) jar peanut butter
1 box confectioners sugar	

Coating:

1 (12 oz.) bar semi-sweet	1/2 bar paraffin wax
chocolate	

Mix margarine and peanut butter. Add sugar gradually. Mix well. Roll into balls to dip in chocolate.

Put chocolate and paraffin wax in top of double boiler. Mix well. Stick toothpick into peanut butter balls for dipping. Leave some area around toothpick undipped to look like a buckeye. Place on wax paper or in small candy wrappers.

Les Carlew

BUTTER CHEWS

3/4 c. butter or oleo	3/4 c. shredded coconut
3 Tbsp. granulated sugar	3 egg whites, beaten
1 1/2 c. flour	1/2 tsp. salt
3 eggs yolks, beaten	2 heaping Tbsp. flour
2 1/4 c. brown sugar (light)	1/2 tsp. baking powder
1/2 c. chopped nuts	1 tsp. vanilla

Cream butter. Add sugar and beat well. Then blend well with the flour. Pat mixture into greased and floured pan, 9 x 12 x 2-inch, and bake in a 375° oven until a delicate brown.

Now add the brown sugar to beaten egg yolks and blend in well. To this, add salt, baking powder, flour and vanilla. Next add nuts and coconut. Then fold in egg whites. Pour this mixture over the baked mixture and return to the oven for 25 to 30 minutes. When cool, ice with Butter Chew Icing.

Butter Chew Icing:

1 stick oleo	grated orange peel zest
3 c. confectioners sugar	roasted salted pecans,
1/4 c. lemon juice	chopped
1/4 c. orange juice	

Cream oleo and confectioners sugar together. Add lemon and orange juice. If too thin, add more confectioners sugar. Spread on cooked Butter Chews. Sprinkle with roasted and salted, chopped nuts.

Margaret L. B. Paydar

CHOCOLATE OAT CHEWIES

1/4 c. butter or margarine	1 tsp. vanilla extract
1/4 c. vegetable oil	1/2 c. all-purpose flour
2/3 c. packed brown sugar	2/3 c. raisins
1 egg, beaten	2/3 c. chopped nuts
1 1/4 c. old-fashioned	2/3 c. semi-sweet chocolate
uncooked rolled oats	chips

Heat oven to 350°. In a medium bowl, blend butter, oil

and brown sugar. Beat in the egg and vanilla until well blended. Stir in oats and flour; mix well. Stir in raisins, nuts and chocolate chips.

Spread batter in lightly greased 8-inch baking pan, or spray pan with cooking spray. Bake for 25 minutes. Cool, then cut into squares.

Store in airtight container. Makes about 2 dozen small squares.

Bebe Schroer

COCONUT CHERRY COOKIES

1 1/4 c. flour	1/2 tsp. salt
1/2 c. sugar	1 egg
1/2 tsp. baking powder	1 c. coconut
1/2 c. butter	1/4 c. chopped cherries

Combine everything but coconut and cherries. Mix well, then stir in coconut and cherries. Bake in 375° oven for 8 to 10 minutes.

These are great at Christmas.

Samantha Tucker

CREAM CHEESE GEMS

1 (3 oz.) pkg. cream cheese	1/2 tsp. vanilla
2 1/2 c. sifted 4x powdered sugar	dash of salt
	walnut or pecan halves

Mix first four ingredients well. Form into nuggets. Place nuts on both sides and secure. Refrigerate until firm.

Peggy Crawford

DATE BALLS

1 stick oleo	1 1/4 c. chopped nuts or
1 c. sugar	2 c. Rice Krispies plus
1 pkg. dates	1/2 c. nuts
1 tsp. vanilla	

Melt oleo, sugar and dates over low heat, being sure sugar dissolves. Add nuts and/or Rice Krispies and vanilla. Form into small balls and roll in Angel Flake coconut. (If the mixture is too sticky to work with, chill it first.)

Margaret L. B. Paydar

NO BAKE CHOCOLATE COOKIES

2 c. sugar
1/2 c. cocoa
1/2 c. milk

1 stick margarine
1/2 c. peanut butter
3 c. quick cook oatmeal

Combine in pan: sugar, cocoa, milk and margarine. Bring to boil and boil 1 minute. Stir in peanut butter and oats. Drop on wax paper and refrigerate. Easy and good.

Samantha Tucker

OATMEAL COCOA BALLS

2 c. sugar
4 Tbsp. cocoa
1 stick butter
1/2 c. milk

2 c. quick oats
1 c. nuts
1/4 tsp. vanilla

Put first 4 ingredients in pot and boil for 2 minutes. Add the last 3 ingredients and stir. Take off heat. Roll into balls and refrigerate.

Peggy Crawford

OATMEAL COOKIES

1 c. margarine
1 c. white sugar
1 c. brown sugar
2 eggs
2 c. oatmeal
2 c. coconut
1 tsp. vanilla

2 c. flour
1 tsp. soda
1 tsp. salt
1 tsp. baking powder
nuts (optional)
chocolate chips (optional)

Cream margarine and sugars. Add eggs. Add flour, soda, salt, baking powder and vanilla and mix well. Mix in oatmeal, coconut, nuts and chocolate chips. Bake at 350° for 10 minutes.

Deborah Geels

PEANUT BUTTER COOKIES

1/2 c. butter or margarine
1/2 c. crunchy peanut butter
1/2 c. white sugar
1/2 c. brown sugar
1 egg

1/2 tsp. vanilla
1/2 tsp. salt
1/2 tsp. baking soda
2 c. flour

Cream together butter or margarine and peanut butter. Beat in sugar and brown sugar. Stir egg, vanilla, salt, baking soda and flour. Arrange by teaspoonfuls on cookie sheet. Press flat with a floured spoon or mark with a floured fork. Bake at 350° until firm, about 10 minutes. Should make about 60.

Peter Dietrich
Jonathan Goree

PEANUT BLOSSOMS

1 (14 oz.) can Eagle Brand
  condensed milk
3/4 c. peanut butter
2 c. Bisquick

1 tsp. vanilla
sugar
1 pkg. Hershey chocolate
  kisses

Preheat oven to 375°.

In large mixing bowl, beat Eagle Brand and peanut butter until smooth. Add Bisquick, gradually, and then add vanilla. Mix well. Shape into 1-inch balls and roll in sugar. Place on an ungreased cookie sheet, 2 inches apart. Bake 6 to 8 minutes or until lightly brown. Remove from oven. While still hot, press chocolate kiss in center of each ball; cool. Makes 5 dozen.

Ruth Anne Talley

PRALINE SQUARES

24 whole graham crackers
1 c. butter or margarine
1 c. brown sugar

1 c. pecans or walnuts,
  chopped

Arrange crackers one layer deep on ungreased cookie sheet or jelly roll pan. Place butter (margarine) and brown sugar in saucepan. Bring to a boil and stir constantly for 2 minutes. Stir in nuts; mix well. Spoon mixture over graham crackers. Bake in 350° oven for 10 minutes. Remove from oven and let stand 2 minutes. Cut into squares while still warm. Store in tins, coffee cans or whatever.

Robin Singleton

S'MORES

1 graham cracker
1 marshmallow
1/2 Hershey bar

a good stick for roasting
  marshmallows
matches
firewood

383391

First build a fire. Get your stick and put the marshmallow on it. Roast until it is done. Break graham cracker in half (2 squares). Put Hershey bar on one of the graham crackers. Put the marshmallow on top of the Hershey bar. Then put the other half of the graham cracker on top. Last: Enjoy!

Karen LeMar

SNICKERDOODLES
(This is an Odd Mennonite Recipe)

1 c. Crisco	2 tsp. baking powder
1/2 c. sugar	1/2 tsp. salt
2 eggs	2 Tbsp. sugar
2 3/4 c. flour	2 tsp. cinnamon

Cream together the Crisco, sugar and eggs. Sift together the flour, baking powder and salt. Blend these together and chill at least one hour. Roll into size of a walnut. Roll balls in a mixture of sugar and cinnamon to coat well. Place 2 inches apart on a greased cookie sheet. Bake at 450° for 8 to 10 minutes until light brown, but soft.

Les Carlew

SPRINKLE COOKIES

1 1/2 sticks margarine (3/4 c.)	1 beaten egg
	2 tsp. vanilla
3/4 c. confectioners sugar	2 c. flour

Cream margarine and sugar. Add beaten egg and vanilla. Mix well. Add flour and mix well again. Drop from a teaspoon onto ungreased cookie sheet. Bake 15 to 20 minutes at 350°. Makes 3 1/2 to 4 dozen.

Heidi Nelson

SUGAR COOKIES

1 pkg. Pillsbury refrigerated sugar cookie dough	wheat germ
	granulated sugar

Slice the refrigerator dough thinly. Sprinkle with wheat germ. Bake as directed on package. Sprinkle with sugar as soon as removed from the oven. Colored sugar may be used for a festive touch.

Margaret L. B. Paydar

SUGAR COOKIES

1 c. powdered sugar
1 c. granulated sugar
2/3 c. butter
1 c. oil
2 eggs

1 tsp. vanilla
4 c. flour plus 1 Tbsp.
1/2 tsp. salt
2/3 tsp. soda
1 tsp. cream of tartar

Cream first 4 ingredients until fluffy. Add the eggs and mix well. Add the vanilla and mix well. Add the dry ingredients to the mixture. Roll into balls and press with bottom of glass. (Spray cookie sheet with Pam.) Bake at 375° for 10 minutes.

Peggy Crawford

THUMBPRINT COOKIES

2 c. flour
1/3 c. sugar
2 sticks butter
1/4 tsp. vanilla

pinch of salt
pinch of baking powder
powdered sugar

Cream butter, sugar, vanilla, salt and baking powder until fluffy. Blend in flour. Shape into balls and press thumb into center. If using self-rising flour, no need for salt or baking powder. Place on ungreased baking sheet, two inches apart. Bake at 350° for about 8 to 10 minutes or until light brown.

Mix about a cup of powdered sugar, a little water and light food coloring until good consistency for icing and spoon into depressed part of cookie.

Paula Moore

BLUEBERRY BREAD PUDDING

1 slice whole wheat bread
1 c. low-fat buttermilk
1 egg
1 Tbsp. sugar

1/2 tsp. vanilla
1/2 c. frozen unsweetened
blueberries

Preheat oven to 350°.

In blender or food processor, combine all ingredients except blueberries. Process until blended. Stir in blueberries. Pour mixture into 1 pint baking dish. Bake one hour or until pudding is set.

Makes one serving with 340 calories. Make this when you make dinner as dessert or save for an easy, ready-to-go breakfast the next morning.

Angela Roberts

MAMAW'S BREAD PUDDING

4 eggs
1 c. sugar
1 qt. milk
1/2 tsp. nutmeg

2 tsp. vanilla
1 (1 lb.) loaf French or
   Italian bread

Mix eggs and sugar thoroughly. Add milk, nutmeg and vanilla and mix with eggs and sugar. Shred bread in small pieces and add to milk mixture.

Grease a 9-inch square pan and pour mixture in. (Can use 13 x 9-inch pan.) Bake at 350° for 1 hour or until golden brown.

Serving suggestions: Serve warm with milk or cream, strawberries or any other juicy fruit, or raspberry jam and whipped cream.

Dawn Brown

FLAN

1 c. sugar
1 (15 oz.) can sweetened
   condensed milk

4 eggs, beaten
1 tsp. flavoring (vanilla)
1 c. water or coffee

Preheat oven to 350°.

Caution! This step is dangerous! Use potholders at all times! Put sugar in deep, flame-proof dish (at least 2 quart capacity) or metal ovenproof pot on low to medium heat, stirring constantly, until sugar melts and turns golden. Tip dish around, using potholders, until it is entirely coated with caramel. Cool while making custard.

Beat together condensed milk, eggs, flavoring and water. Pour into caramel-coated dish. Place dish in larger pan containing hot water and bake 1 hour or until tester comes out clean. Cool at room temperature 30 minutes, then in refrigerator at least 2 hours. When ready to serve, invert dish onto platter.

Optional: Before serving, pour brandy or rum over flan, light, and send to table flaming.

Jon Katze

GLAZEE' FRUIT

1 (4 serving size) vanilla
   instant pudding
1 large can chunk pineapple

1 can mandarin oranges
2 to 3 bananas, sliced

Stir the juice from the pineapple and oranges into the pudding mix, reserving a small amount to coat the banana slices to prevent darkening. It will glaze.

Fold in fruit. Chill. Serve for brunch or makes a lovoly dessert. Delicious!

Bettylu Meier
Grandmother of Tori and
Alex Rodriguez

HOMEMADE ICE CREAM

1 can Eagle Brand
1/2 c. sugar
6 eggs

2 Tbsp. vanilla
1/2 gal. milk

Separate eggs. Beat egg whites until stiff.

Add to egg yolks: Eagle Brand, sugar, vanilla and 1/4 of milk. Mix well. Pour into ice cream freezer container. Add remaining milk. Fold in egg whites and freeze.

Leigh Kendrick

NA-NA'S SPECIAL DESSERT

1 qt. whipped cream
2 (8 oz.) pkg. cream cheese

2 (11 oz.) cans mandarin
   oranges, drained
sugar to taste

Whip cream. Add sugar to taste. Cream the cheese with small amount of whipped cream, then slowly fold in whipped cream. Gently fold in orange slices. Serve in sherbet glasses. Delicious.

Bettylu Meier,
Grandmother (Na-Na) of
Alex and Tori Rodriguez

STRAWBERRIES ITALIANE

5 Tbsp. balsamic vinegar
2 Tbsp. sugar
3/4 Tbsp. ground pepper

5 c. strawberries, washed,
dried and halved
2 Tbsp. grated orange rind
(optional)

Mix first three ingredients in a bowl or food processor. Add berries and refrigerate at least 20 minutes.

Great with ice cream, pound cake, ladyfingers or angel food cake.

Sara Lyras

RITA'S BEST NOODLE PUDDING

1 lb. pkg. broad noodles
1 large can fruit cocktail
with juice
5 large eggs, beaten until frothy

1 c. white raisins
1 c. sugar
1 tsp. almond extract

Topping:

1/2 c. crushed cornflakes
1/3 c. pecan pieces

2 tsp. cinnamon
1 Tbsp. sugar

Boil noodles until done. Drain and put into large bowl. Add remaining ingredients except topping.

In 8 x 13-inch baking pan, melt 1/2 cup oil with 1/2 cup shortening. Pour half of this mixture into noodle mixture, leaving rest in pan. Mix well and pour into pan. Top with topping mixture. Bake at 350° for one hour.

High fat, cholesterol and calories here! Freezes well.

Vicki Less

OATMEAL COOKIES

1 c. Crisco
3/4 c. brown sugar (not granulated, not light, but real brown sugar)
1 1/4 c. granulated sugar
1 tsp. soda (fresh)
1 tsp. baking powder
3 tsp. cinnamon

2 tsp. vanilla
3 c. chopped pecans
3 eggs
1 c. flour
1/4 tsp. salt
2 tsp. nutmeg
3 3/4 c. quick Quaker oatmeal

Cream shortening and sugars thoroughly. Add eggs and vanilla; cream. Sift dry ingredients together. Gradually add to creamed mixture. Add oatmeal and pecans. Let sit for 5 minutes to allow oatmeal to absorb moisture.

Bake at 350° for 12 to 15 minutes. Cool 2 or 3 minutes and remove from cookie sheet to wire rack to cool. Cookies will puff and crack on surface and no moisture will appear under cracks.

Patty Calvert

<<< Extra Recipes >>>

<<< Extra Recipes >>>

Helpful Cooking Hints

Frozen gravies or sauces may be a little thicker after thawing than when they were freshly made. Adding a little appropriate liquid — milk, broth, bouillon or wine — will thin them to the desired consistency.

For extra juicy, extra nutritious hamburgers, add ¼ cup evaporated milk per pound of meat before shaping.

To ripen green pears, just place 2 or 3 in a brown bag, loosely closed, and store at room temperature out of direct sunlight.

In making pickles, use white vinegar to make clear pickles and coarse salt which comes in 5 pound bags. This is not rock salt. Avoid using iodized salt for pickle making. Most pickles are better if allowed to stand six weeks before using.

Lemon gelatine dissolved in 2 cups of hot apricot nectar with 1 teaspoon of grated lemon added for zip makes a perfect base for jellied fruit salad.

Put a tablespoon of butter in the water when cooking rice, dried beans, macaroni, to keep it from boiling over. Always run cold water over it when done to get the starch out. Reheat over hot water, if necessary.

A pair of scissors (not the fowl kind — they are heavy and awkward to handle) fine for slivering celery, onion, meats, and cheese.

Never put a cover on anything that is cooked in milk unless you want to spend hours cleaning up the stove when it boils over.

Anything that grows under the ground start off in cold water — potatoes, beets, carrots, etc. Anything that grows above ground, start off in boiling water — English peas, greens, beans, etc.

To clean aluminum pots when they are stained dark, merely boil with a little cream of tartar, vinegar or acid foods.

Baking powder will remove tea or coffee stains from china pots or cups.

Learn where your fuse box and master cut-off switch is. If you know where the lever is to pull you can always cut the current off until a service man can come.

Canned cream soups make excellent sauces for vegetables, fish, etc. Celery with lobster, black bean or onion with cauliflower, tomato with lamb chops.

Slip your hand inside a waxed sandwich bag and you have a perfect mitt for greasing your baking pans and casserole dishes.

To reheat roast, wrap in aluminum foil and heat in a slow oven.

Hard boiled eggs will peel easily when cracked and placed in cold water immediately after taking out of the hot water.

You can cut a meringue pie cleanly by coating both sides of the knife lightly with butter.

When recipe calls for adding raw eggs to hot mixture, always begin by adding a small amount of hot mixture to the beaten eggs slowly to avoid curdling.

To remove fish odor from hands, utensils and dish cloths, use one teaspoon baking soda to quart of water.

To keep icings moist and to prevent cracking, add a pinch of baking soda to the icing.

If soup tastes very salty, a raw piece of potato placed in the pot will absorb the salt.

Pour water into mold and then drain before pouring in mixture to be chilled. Will come out of mold easier.

When rolling cooky dough, sprinkle board with powdered sugar instead of flour. Too much flour makes the dough heavy. When freezing cookies with a frosting, place them in freezer unwrapped for about 2 hours — then wrap without worrying about them sticking together.

TROPICAL DELIGHT
(Beverage)

2 bananas, sliced and frozen
2/3 c. orange juice

2/3 c. plain yogurt
ice cubes

Combine first 3 ingredients in container of an electric blender. Add enough ice cubes to bring mixture to 2 1/2 cups level. Blend until smooth. Serve immediately. Makes 2 drinks.

Donna Funcke

APPLE HOT SPOT

3 c. apple juice
6 orange slices

1 (24 oz.) bottle unsweetened
   white grape juice

In a saucepan, mix fruit juices. Warm juices over low heat. Pour into cups. Makes 12 (4 ounce) servings.

Bonnie & Christopher Churchwell

BANANA PUNCH
(Serves 75 (4 oz.) cups)

4 c. sugar
6 c. water
6 oz. frozen orange juice
   concentrate

2 Tbsp. ReaLemon
46 oz. can pineapple juice
5 bananas
5 qt. ginger ale

Cook sugar and water. Let boil 3 minutes and cool. Pulverize bananas in blender. To this add lemon juice and orange juice. Mix pineapple juice, sugar and water mixture and bananas. Pour into 1/2 gallon milk carton and freeze.

About 30 minutes before serving, put frozen punch into bowl and pour ginger ale over it. Mix to form a slush.

Les Carlew

BOILED CUSTARD

1 qt. sweet milk
4 eggs
1 c. sugar

1 tsp. vanilla
1 1/2 pt. whipping cream
nutmeg

Beat eggs and sugar together in a blender until smooth

and creamy. Stir in milk and cook in a gallon glass jar placed in a 5 quart pan, filled with water, almost to the top. Stir constantly until it begins to thicken, over low heat.

When it begins to coat a spoon, remove from heat and cool. Beat in vanilla. Strain. Beat whipping cream, to be added when served. Sprinkle with nutmeg on top.

Sherry Hulen

CITRUS WINE WELCOMER

2 c. orange juice
1 (6 oz.) can frozen lemonade
   concentrate, thawed
1 c. Cointreau or other
   orange-flavored liqueur

1 (25.4 oz.) bottle dry white
   wine, chilled
1 liter club soda, chilled
crushed ice
orange slices

Combine first 4 ingredients in a punch bowl. Stir. Add club soda and crushed ice, stirring gently.

Garnish with orange slices. Serves 10 to 12.

Sherry Hulen

CRANBERRY PUNCH

4 c. cranberry juice
1 1/2 c. sugar
4 c. pineapple juice
1 Tbsp. almond extract

2 liter ginger ale
fresh fruit slices
rum (optional)

Combine first 4 ingredients. Stir until sugar is dissolved. Chill. Add ginger ale just before serving. Garnish with fruit slices if desired. Rum, in any amount, can be added to this punch. Serves 30.

Sherry Hulen

FROZEN MARGARITAS

1 (6 oz.) can frozen limeade
9 oz. tequila
2 oz. Triple Sec

1/8 lime, diced
coarse salt

Put first four ingredients in blender. Fill with ice and blend until smooth. Rub edge of glass with lime and dip in coarse salt. Pour margaritas into glass and serve.

Sherry Hulen

FRUIT PUNCH

1/2 gal. orange sherbet
1 large can Pet milk
1 can Hawaiian punch (mixed fruit)

1/2 gal. pineapple sherbet
2 bottles ginger ale

Soften in large container both sherbets. Mix with milk and punch. When ready to serve, add ale.

Sherry Hulen

HONEY LIMEADE

2 Tbsp. honey ice cubes
2/3 c. sugar

5 c. water
1 c. reconstituted lime juice

Pour the lime juice in the pitcher. Add the water, honey and sugar. Stir until sugar is dissolved. Refrigerate until ready to serve. Put several ice cubes in each glass. Pour limeade over the ice cubes in the glasses. Makes 6 (8 ounce) servings.

Bonne & Christopher Churchwell

INSTANT COCOA

8 qt. box dry milk
6 to 7 oz. coffee creamer
1/2 Tbsp. salt

8 oz. Nestle Quik
2 c. powdered sugar

Mix and store. Use 1/2 cup mix per 1 cup hot water.

Heidi Nelson

KIDS FRUIT PUNCH

2 (12 oz.) cans frozen orange
   juice concentrated

1 1/2 c. unsweetened
   pineapple juice
4 c. apple juice

Prepare orange juice according to directions. Mix with pineapple juice and apple juice. Serve chilled. Serves 24.

Sherry Hulen

PERCOLATOR PUNCH

3 c. pineapple juice
3 c. cranberry juice

1 1/2 c. water

In Basket of Percolator:

1/3 c. brown sugar	1 stick cinnamon
1 1/2 tsp. whole cloves	

Mix juices together. Put in percolator. Put spices in top of basket and perk. Makes 10 cups.

Becky Cunningham

PIMM'S CUP

48 oz. ginger ale	12 slices lime
24 oz. ginger beer	12 (6 x 1/2-inch) cucumber
1 1/3 c. Pimm's #1	sticks

Mix first three ingredients. Place ice in tall glass. Pour in mixture. Garnish with lime and cucumber.

Martha Brahm

SPICE TEA MIX

2 c. Tang	1 tsp. ground cloves
1 small pkg. lemonade (dry)	1 tsp. cinnamon
1 1/2 c. sugar	1/2 tsp. nutmeg
3/4 c. instant tea	

Mix and store in an airtight container. Use 2 teaspoons per cup hot water.

Heidi Nelson
Avis Bradley

SPICED WASSAIL

6 small apples	1 tsp. whole cloves
1 c. brown sugar	1 tsp. whole allspice,
1 c. brandy	crushed
2 c. water	2 (750 milliliters) red wine
12 inch stick cinnamon	1 (750 milliliters) sherry

Core apples; place in baking dish with all ingredients except wine and sherry. Cover with foil and bake 30 to 40 minutes or until apples are soft.

Heat wine and sherry. Pour into punch. Boil mix with melted sugar and spices from baking dish. Float in apples and serve.

Martha Brahm

WEDDING PUNCH

3 c. sugar
6 c. water
1 (12 oz.) frozen orange
  juice
6 oz. concentrated lemon
  juice (bottled)

1 (46 oz.) can pineapple
  juice
5 bananas
2 cartons frozen strawberries
2 Tbsp. pineapple juice

Heat and dissolve sugar and water. Remove and cool. Add next 3 ingredients. Put bananas and strawberries in blender with 2 tablespoons pineapple juice. Mix all together. Pour into 2 1/2 gallon plastic containers and freeze. (Do not fill to top; allow for expansion.)

Two hours before serving, remove from freezer and thaw slightly. To each 1/2 gallon use 2 bottles ginger ale. (Makes a slush.) Can be colored with cake coloring to fit occasion. Serves 50 to 75.

Mrs. Allen Hewitt

CINNAMON PECANS

1 c. sugar
1 tsp. cinnamon
1/4 tsp. salt

2 c. pecan halves
1 tsp. vanilla
6 Tbsp. milk

Mix first three ingredients, then add milk. Stir and bring to a boil. Cook to a soft ball stage. Add vanilla. Stir. Pour in nut halves and stir until well coated. Turn out on wax paper and separate with two forks or fingers.

Note: A nice gift.

Bettylu Meier,
Grandmother of Alex and
Tori Rodriguez

ELEPHANT STEW

1 medium-sized elephant
1 ton salt
1 ton pepper
500 bushels potatoes

200 bushels carrots
4000 sprigs parsley
2 small rabbits (optional)

Cut elephant meat into bite-size pieces. This will take two months. Cut veggies into cubes (another 2 months). Place meat in pan and cover with 1000 gallons of gravy and simmer for 4 weeks. Shovel in salt and pepper to taste. When meat is tender, add veggies. A steam shovel is useful for this. Simmer slowly for 4 more weeks.

Garnish with parsley. Will serve 3800 people. If more people are expected, add rabbits. This is not recommended as very few people like hare in their stew.

Cathay Fleming

EVA'S CHOCOLATE COVERED BRITTLE

1 c. margarine or butter	6 oz. chocolate chips
1/2 lb. sugar (1 1/4 c.)	1/4 to 1/2 c. chopped pecans

Melt butter on medium-high heat. Add sugar. Stir 15 to 20 minutes until mixture turns the color of peanut butter. Spread mixture onto a greased cookie sheet. Spread real thin with knife. Sprinkle chocolate chips and spread all over brittle. Sprinkle nuts and freeze until hard. Break apart to serve.

Joy Stubbs

HAM AND AVOCADO CORONETS

1 avocado, peeled and chopped	1/4 c. raw peanuts
juice of one lemon	salt and pepper to taste
2 hard-cooked eggs	1/4 tsp. cayenne pepper
1 tomato, chopped	1/2 bunch parsley, chopped
1/2 onion, diced finely	8 leaves lettuce (for
6 (1/8-inch thick) slices ham	garnish)

Ginger Basil Mayonnaise:

2 Tbsp. fresh ginger	1 c. mayonnaise
1 Tbsp. fresh basil or 1 tsp. dried	

Combine chopped avocado with lemon juice. Toss well and add eggs, tomato, onion and raw peanuts. Add salt and pepper to taste. Add a dash of cayenne pepper for a little extra spice.

In a separate bowl, mix the Ginger Basil Mayonnaise. Use all but 8 teaspoons of the mayonnaise mixture to bind the salad stuffing. Place 1/8 of the stuffing on a slice of ham and roll into a coronet shape. Place a lettuce leaf on a plate. On top of this, place the ham coronet and dab 1 teaspoon of mayonnaise on top.

If you prefer, you can substitute plain mayo for Ginger Basil Mayonnaise. Serves 6.

**Martha Brahm,
Fascinating Foods**

HOT DOG

hot dog   bun

Put in the microwave for one minute.

Alan Giles

KENTUCKY HOT BROWNS

4 Tbsp. margarine
1 onion, chopped
1/3 c. all-purpose flour
1 Tbsp. cornstarch
3 c. milk
1 tsp. salt
1/2 tsp. cayenne pepper
6 oz. Velveeta cheese, cubed

2 eggs, beaten
8 English muffin halves
1 lb. sliced turkey
8 slices bacon, cooked and
   crumbled
Parmesan cheese
paprika

Melt 3 tablespoons margarine in saucepan. Add onion and saute until clear and tender. Add flour; stir thoroughly. Heat milk in microwave in glass measuring cup just until warm. Add to flour mixture, gradually, stirring thoroughly. Add salt and pepper. Stir constantly until thickened. Add cheese. Stir until melted.

Stir about 1/2 cup of the hot mixture into eggs. Then put back into main pan. Put English muffin halves onto baking sheet. Top with turkey, cheese sauce, bacon, Parmesan and paprika. Broil for 4 to 5 minutes.

Served in Kentucky state parks and resorts.

J. Whitson

POPCORN

Put some popcorn seeds in a bowl and put it in the microwave for 2 minutes.

Alan Giles

POPSICLES

1 bottle Welch's cherry juice
1 bottle apple juice

paper cups and popsicle
   sticks or popsicle molds

383391

Mix cherry juice with apple juice in a 2 to 1 ratio. Pour into desired number of cups. Put into freezer. When partially frozen, add sticks. Or, do what I do, and buy the molds that have the stick built into the top.

You can use any flavor juice with the apple but cherry is my favorite.

Michelle Kennedy

ANTS ON A LOG

celery   raisins
peanut butter

Cut celery in half. Spread peanut butter on celery. Put raisins on top.

Gary Bell

SKEENBURGERS
(Also Very Easy)

5 lb. ground chuck   3 tsp. Tabasco
1 c. applesauce   5 Tbsp. Worcestershire sauce
1 c. Ritz crackers, crumbled   1 envelope Lipton onion soup
5 tsp. Accent   salt to taste

Combine all ingredients. Cook on medium heat on grill.

Susan Moon Weaver

STRAWBERRIES WITH POWDERED SUGAR

strawberries   powdered sugar

Put strawberries in bowl and add powdered sugar.

Kori Bell

SQUEEZED PEANUT BUTTER AND JELLY SANDWICH

bread   jelly
peanut butter

First get the bread. Then get the peanut butter. Then spread it on the sandwich. Then get the jelly. Then spread it on the sandwich. Then close it up and eat.

Jesse Vance

FINGER PAINT 1

1/2 c. starch
1 qt. boiling water
1/2 c. soap flakes
1/4 c. talcum powder

poster paint or finely ground
    colored chalk
oil of clove

Soften starch in a small amount of cold water. Over medium-low heat, add boiling water, stirring constantly, until mixture bubbles. Remove from heat. Let it cool and add soap flakes and powder. Stir until well mixed.

Pour into containers, one for each color and stir in color pigment. Add a few drops of oil of clove to prevent distressing odors.

Sherry Hulen

PLAYDOUGH

1 c. flour
1/2 c. salt
2 tsp. cream of tartar

1 c. water
1 tsp. oil

Mix together. Cook on medium-high until balls form (less than 10 minutes). Knead when cool to get desired texture. Work with your hands. Divide to make different colors before adding food coloring. Wear rubber gloves to prevent food coloring from staining hands.

Lynette Clemmons

MICRO COOKIE KRISPS

1 c. light corn syrup
1 c. white sugar
1 c. peanut butter

2 c. corn flakes
2 c. Rice Krispies

Melt first 3 ingredients in microwave until hot. Do not boil. Add cereal. Put in a 9-inch square, greased pan. Cool. Cut into bars.

MICROWAVE FUDGE

3 c. milk chocolate chips
1 (14 oz.)can sweetened
    condensed milk

1/4 c. margarine
1 c. walnuts

Place all ingredients except nuts in large microwave safe bowl. Microwave at Medium until chocolate chips are melted, 3 to 5 minutes. Pour into well-greased square baking dish, 8 x 8-inches. Refrigerate until set.

Heidi Nelson

HOT AND SPICY NUTS

2 Tbsp. olive oil
2 tsp. garlic salt
2 lb. can mixed nuts

1 (5/8 oz.) pkg. chili
  seasoning mix
2 tsp. extra hot chili powder

Heat oil with garlic salt. Add nuts. Reduce heat and toss, using two spoons, until nuts are well coated. Pour into large bowl. Blend chili seasoning and powder. Add to nuts. Mix until nuts are well coated.

Store in airtight container.

Donna Davis

<<< Extra Recipes >>>

INDEX

BREADS, ROLLS & PASTRIES

CAKES, COOKIES & DESSERTS

BEVERAGES, MICROWAVE & MISCELLANEOUS

Your's free!

Now you're invited to have
Fundcraft's New Sampler Cookbook

It's filled with an exciting selection of recipes, colorful section dividers, cover designs and many other tips for publishing your very own custom cookbook at the lowest cost ever!

Raise $5000.00 or more for your church, school or organization.

Fundcraft's time-tested plan allows you to offer a beautiful, professionally-done cookbook that everyone will love. So beautiful in fact, that priced at two to three times your cost, it's still a bargain! It will have a complete recipe index. And, if you wish, a full color cover and section dividers. Smart buyers will want several as gifts.

No investment or risk.

Fundcraft trusts you to make payment 37 days after you receive your books. Your success is guaranteed, so there's no worry about cost. Fundcraft knows that

friends, neighbors, relatives will be thrilled to buy your cookbooks. Recipes are submitted by your members, whose names appear right along side. Your organization name is on the cover and several inside pages. So your cookbook is PERSONALIZED throughout, and not available anywhere else.

Our exclusive "recipe for success."

Fundcraft has been publishing community cookbooks since 1942, and we're still getting better. We help you every step of the way so that you and your members have FUN while doing a constructive service for your community.

Return this card for your free cookbook and full information.
(Tear along perforation, fill in and mail)

Dear Fundcraft:
    Please send my copy of your Sampler Cookbook and complete information for publishing our own community cookbook. I am assured there's no obligation.

Organization_____ No. of Members_____

Your Name_____

Address_____

City_____ State_____ Zip_____

For immediate information call **TOLL-FREE 1-800-351-7822**
(In Tennessee, call 901-853-7070)

Publish Your Own Cookbook
With Hometown Recipes!

If you belong to an organization that needs money, return this postage-paid card TODAY for our low cost, guaranteed cookbook fundraising plan. All you do is collect the recipes from group members and FUNDCRAFT DOES THE REST!

For even faster service, call
TOLL-FREE 1-800-351-7822
(In Tennessee call 901-853-7070)

Professional Cookbooks on a Fundraising Budget!

052-F   (Tear along perforation, fill in other side and mail)

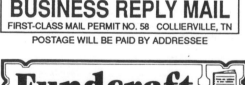

"Little Known"
HOUSEHOLD HINTS

. . . that even your Grandmother probably didn't know!

GENERAL

- Rubbing alcohol will remove ball-point pen ink marks.
- Candles chilled for 24 hours in refrigerator will burn longer and not drip.
- Baking soda on a damp cloth will remove grime and grease from glass on oven door.
- Window cleaner will clean and polish exterior of appliances — stove, refrigerator — also small appliances, taps, etc.
- Mixture of half salt and half hot vinegar rubbed on brass will clean and polish.
- To re-smooth Teflon pans, boil for 5 to 10 minutes in the pan, a mixture of 1 cup water, 2 tablespoons baking soda, 1/2 cup liquid bleach. Wash in suds and rinse thoroughly. Then before using, wipe the surface with salad oil.
- To remove gum from hair, rub a plain chocolate bar in hair — then wash.
- A cloth wrung out of a solution of 1 tablespoon cornstarch dissolved in one quart of water, will make windows and mirrors sparkle.
- Cold tea, coffee grounds, or egg shells make a good fertilizer for house plants and act as insecticides, too.
- Try waxing your ashtrays. Ashes won't cling, odors won't linger and they can be wiped clean with a paper towel or disposable tissue. This saves daily washing.
- Stamp a few moth balls into the ground near flower beds to keep dogs away.

continued

...and more
"Little Known"
HOUSEHOLD HINTS

- To save mess in making bread or graham cracker crumbs, place in plastic bag and roll with rolling pin.
- Add a little salad oil in when you cook macaroni or spaghetti and it will not boil over or stick.

VINEGAR

- A bowl of vinegar placed in a stuffy or smokey room will absorb tobacco smoke or the smell of paint, and keep the air fresh.

MILK

- Rinse pan with cold water before heating milk in it to prevent scorching and make cleaning easier.
- To make sour milk from sweet milk, add 1 tablespoon vinegar or lemon juice to 1 cup sweet milk.

PIES

- When baking fruit pies, cut holes in the upper crust with a thimble, place crust on pie. The holes will become larger, then place the little round circles back in place. Makes pies very decorative and serves for the steam and juice openings.
- Make your two-crust pies the night before you need them. Put in refrigerator overnight. In the morning take from refrigerator. Let pie warm to room temperature, if in glassware, so the glass won't break. Bake as usual.
- Put cream or milk on top of two-crust pies for a nice brown pie.
- Put a layer of marshmallows in the bottom of a pumpkin pie, then add the filling. You will have a nice topping as the marshmallows will come to the top.
- Cut drinking straws into short lengths and insert through slits in pie crusts to prevent juice from running over in the oven and permit steam to escape.

ABBREVIATIONS COMMONLY USED

tsp. - teaspoon
Tbsp. - tablespoon
c. - cup
pt. - pint
qt. - quart
pk. - peck
bu. - bushel

oz. - ounce or ounces
lb. - pound or pounds
sq. - square
min. - minute or minutes
hr. - hour or hours
mod. - moderate or moderately
doz. - dozen

SIMPLIFIED MEASURES

dash - less than 1/8 teaspoon
3 teaspoons - 1 tablespoon
16 tablespoons - 1 cup
1 cup - 1/2 pint
2 cups -1 pint

2 pints (4 cups) - 1 quart
4 quarts (liquid) - 1 gallon
8 quarts (solid) - 1 peck
4 pecks - 1 bushel
16 ounces - 1 pound

If you want to measure part-cups by the tablespoon, remember:
4 tablespoons -1/4 cup
5 1/3 tablespoons - 1/3 cup
8 tablespoons - 1/2 cup

10 2/3 tablespoons - 2/3 cup
12 tablespoons -3/4 cup
14 tablespoons - 7/8 cup

OVEN TEMPERATURES

Slow ....250 to 300 Degrees
Slow moderate 325
Moderate 350
Quick moderate 375
Moderately hot 400
Hot ....425 to 450
Very Hot ....475 to 500

CONTENTS OF CANS

Of the different sizes of cans used by commercial canners, the most common are:

Size	Average Contents
8 oz.	1 cup
picnic	1 1/4 cups
#300	1 3/4 cups
No. 1 tall	2 cups
No. 303	2 cups
No. 2	2 1/2 cups
No. 2 1/2	3 1/2 cups
No. 3	4 cups
No. 10	12 to 13 cups

Helpful Cooking Hints

TERMS
Used in Cooking

APPETIZER   A small serving of food served before or as the first course of a meal.

ASPIC   A transparent jelly, usually meat, which has been boiled down to become firm when cold.

BATTER   A mixture of flour or liquid that can be beaten or stirred.

BISQUE   A rich thick cream soup made from fish.

BLANCH   To place fruits or nuts in boiling water to remove skins, also to dip vegetables in boiling water in preparation for freezing, canning or drying.

BOUILLABAISE   A chowder made from several varieties of fish and wine.

BOUILLON   Clear soup made from lean beef or chicken.

BRAISE   To brown meat or vegetables in hot fat, then to cook slowly in small amount of liquid.

CARAMEL   Burnt sugar syrup used for coloring and flavoring. Also a chewy candy.

CHICORY   A plant root that is cut into slices, dried and roasted into coffee. The plant leaves are used for salad and sometimes call curly endive.

CIDER   The juice from pressed apples used as a beverage or to make vinegar.

CLARIFY   To make a liquid clear by adding beaten egg white and egg shells. The egg coagulates in hot liquid and cloudiness adheres to it. The liquid is then strained.

COBBLER   A fruit pie with a rich biscuit dough made in a deep-dish.

COCKTAIL   An appetizer served before or as the first course of a meal. An alcoholic beverage served before the dinner; or cut shellfish with tart sauce served at the start of a meal.

CRACKLINGS   Crisp particles left after fat has been fried out.

CROQUETTES	Chopped meat held together by eggs, shaped and dipped into crumbs, then fried.
DOUGH	A mixture of flour and liquid that is stiff enough to be kneaded.
DRIPPINGS	Liquids resulting from meat being cooked.
ENTREE	The main course of a meal.
FONDUE	A dish made of cheese, eggs, etc.
FRITTERS	Vegetables or fruit covered with batter then fried in deep fat.
FROSTING	A sugar that has been cooked and used to cover cakes, and other foods.
GIBLETS	The liver, gizzard or heart of poultry.
GINGER	An aromatic, pungent root sold fresh, dried or ground. May be used in pickles, preserves, cakes, cookies, puddings, soups, pot roasts.
GLACE	Ice or glossed over. Meats are glazed by covering with concentrated stocks or jellies.
GRATE	Cut into tiny particles, using small holes of grater
HORS d'OEUVRES	Tart, salty or crisp foods served as appetizers.
INFUSION	Liquid extracted from tea, herbs or coffee.
JULIENNE	Cut in fine strips or strings.
KNEAD	To place dough on flat surface and work it, pressing down with knuckles, then fold over, repeating several times.
LEGUMES	The seeds of certain plants, as peas, beans, peanuts, and lentils.
MACEDOINE	A mixture of fruits or vegetables.
MARJORAM	May be used both green and dry for flavoring soups and ragouts, and in stuffing for all meats and fish.
MARINATE	Let food stand in liquid that will add flavor or tenderize.
MINCE	To cut foods in very fine pieces.
MORNAY	A white sauce containing cheese.
OREGANO	Whole or ground, strong aromatic odor, used with tomato sauces, pizza and veal dishes.
SHRED	Cut into thin pieces, using large holes of grater or shredder (cheese).

PARE	Cut off outer covering with a knife or other sharp tool (potatoes, apples).
PEEL	Strip off outer covering (oranges).
PIQUANT	A sharp sauce.
SCALD	Heat milk to just below the boiling point. Tiny bubbles form at edge.
SIMMER	Cook in liquid just below the boiling point. Bubbles form slowly and collapse below the surface.
TARRAGON	Leaves have a hot, pungent taste. Valuable to use in all salads and sauces. Used to flavor vinegar.

FOOD PROCESSES

BAKE	To cook by dry heat, usually in an oven.
BARBECUE	To roast or broil whole, as a hog, fowl, etc. Usually done in a revolving frame over coals or upright in front of coals. To cook thin slices of meat in a highly seasoned vinegar sauce.
BOIL	To cook in liquid, usually water, in which large bubbles rise rapidly and continually so that all the liquid is agitated.
BOILING POINT	The temperature reached when a mixture maintains a full bubbling motion on its surface.
BREW	To cook in hot liquid until flavor is extracted.
BROIL	To cook by exposing the food directly to the heat.
BRAISE	To cook meat by searing in fat, then simmering in a covered dish in small amount of moisture.
CANDY	To conserve or preserve by boiling with sugar. To incrust or coat with sugar.
COATSPOON	When a mixture forms a thin even film on the spoon.
CODDLE	To cook slowly and gently in a liquid just below the boiling point.
CREAM	To beat until soft and fluffy. Usually applied to shortening and sugar.
CUBE	To cut in even sized pieces.
CUT	To divide foods with a knife or scissors.
DICE	To cut into small cubes.
DISSOLVE	To pass into solution.
FOLD	To combine, using a motion beginning vertically down through the mixture, continuing across the bottom of the bowl and ending with an upward and over motion.

CALORIE COUNTER

CANDIES, SNACKS AND NUTS

Calories

Almonds (salted)	12 to 15	93
Cashews	6 to 8	88
Chocolate Bar (nut)	2 ounce bar	340
Coconut (Shredded)	1 cup	344
English Toffee	1 piece	25
Fudge	1 ounce	115
Mints	5 very small	50
Peanuts (salted)	1 ounce	190
Peanuts (roasted)	1 cup	800
Pecans	6	104
Popcorn (plain)	1 cup	54
Potato Chips	10 medium chips	115
Pretzels	10 small sticks	35
Walnuts	8 to 10	100

DAIRY PRODUCTS

American Cheese	1 cube, $1\frac{1}{8}$ inch	100
Butter or Oleomargarine	1 level Tbsp.	100
Cheese (blue, cheddar, cream, Swiss)	1 ounce	105
Cottage Cheese (uncreamed)	1 ounce	25
Cream, light	1 Tbsp.	30
Cream, whipped	1 Tbsp.	25
Egg White	1	15
Egg Yolk	1	61
Eggs (boiled or poached)	2	160
Eggs (scrambled)	2	220
Egg (fried)	1 medium	110
Yogurt (flavored)	4 ounces	60

DESSERTS

Cakes;

Angel Food Cake	2" piece	110
Cheese Cake	2" piece	200
Chocolate Cake, iced	2" piece	445
Fruit Cake	2" piece	115
Pound Cake	1 ounce piece	140
Sponge Cake	2" piece	120
Shortcake with fruit	1 ave. slice	300
Cupcake, iced	1	185
Cupcake, plain	1	145

Pudding:

Bread Pudding	½ cup	150
Flavored Puddings	½ cup	140

Pies:

Apple	1 piece	331
Blueberry	1 piece	290
Cherry	1 piece	355
Custard	1 piece	280
Lemon Meringue	1 piece	305
Peach	1 piece	280

Helpful Cooking Hints

CALORIE COUNTER
DESSERTS (cont.)

		Calories
Pumpkin	1 piece	265
Rhubarb	1 piece	265

Ice Cream:
Chocolate Ice Cream	½ cup	200
Vanilla Ice Cream	½ cup	150

Miscellaneous:
Chocolate Eclair, custard	1 small	250
Cookies, assorted	1, 3-inch dia.	120
Cream Puff	1	296
Jello, all flavors	½ cup	78

BEVERAGES AND JUICES

Beer	1 bottle, 12 oz.	185
Chocolate Malted	8 ounces	450
Cocoa (all milk)	8 ounces	235
Cocoa (milk & water)	8 ounces	140
Coffee (black/unsw.)		0

BREADS AND FLOUR FOODS

Baking Powder Biscuits	1 large or 2 sm.	129
Bran Muffin	1 medium	106
Corn Bread	1 small square	130
Dumplings	1 medium	70
Enriched White Bread	1 slice	60
French Bread	1 small slice	54
French Toast	1 slice	135
Macaroni and Cheese	1 cup	475
Melba Toast	1 slice	25
Noodles cooked	1 cup	200
Pancakes (wheat)	1, 4-inch	60
Raisin Bread	1 slice	80
Rye Bread	1 slice	71
Saltines	1	17
Soda Crackers	1	23
Waffles	1	216
Whole Wheat Bread	1 slice	55

BREAKFAST CEREALS

Corn Flakes	1 cup	96
Cream of Wheat	1 cup	120
Oatmeal	1 cup	148
Rice Flakes	1 cup	105
Shredded Wheat	1 biscuit	100
Sugar Krisps	¾ cup	110

FISH AND FOWL

Bass	4 ounces	105
Brook Trout	4 ounces	130
Crabmeat (canned)	3 ounces	85
Fish Sticks	5 sticks or 4 oz.	200
Haddock (baked)	1 fillet	158
Haddock (broiled)	4 ounces (steak)	207

Helpful Cooking Hints

CALORIE COUNTER
FRUITS

		Calories
Apple (raw)	1 small	70
Banana	1 medium	85
Blueberries (frozen/unsweetened)	½ cup	45
Cantaloupe Melon	½ melon large	60
Cherries, fresh/whole	½ cup	40
Cranberries (sauce)	1 cup	54
Grapes	1 cup	65
Dates	3 or 4	95
Grapefruit (unsw.)	½	55
Orange	1 medium	70
Peach (fresh)	1	35
Plums	2	50
Tangerine (fresh)	1	40
Watermelon	1" slice	60

MEATS

Bacon (crisp)	2 slices	95
Frankfurter	1	155
Hamburger (ave. fat/broiled)	3 ounces	245
Hamburger (lean/broiled)	3 ounces	185
Ham (boiled/lean)	3 ounces	200
Ham (baked)	1 slice	100
Lamb Leg Roast	3 ounces	235
Lamb Chop (rib)	3 ounces	300
Liver (fried)	3½ ounces	210
Meat Loaf	1 slice	100
Pork Chop (med.)	3 ounces	340
Pork Roast	3 ounces	310
Pork Sausage	3 ounces	405
Roasts (Beef)		
Loin Roast	3½ ounces	340
Pot Roast (round)	3½ ounces	200
Rib Roast	3½ ounces	260
Rump Roast	3½ ounces	340
Spareribs	1 piece, 3 ribs	123
Swiss Steak	3½ ounces	300
Veal Chop (med.)	3 ounces	185
Veal Roast	3 ounces	230

SALADS AND DRESSINGS

Apple and Carrot (no dressing)	½ cup	100
Chef Salad/reg. oil	1 Tbsp.	160
Chef Salad/mayonnaise	1 Tbsp.	125
Chef Salad/French, Roquefort	1 Tbsp.	105
Cole Slaw (no dressing)	½ cup	102
Fruit Gelatin	1 square	139
Potato Salad (no dressing)	½ cup	184
Waldorf (no dressing)	½ cup	140
Boiled Dressing	1 Tbsp.	28
French Dressing	1 Tbsp.	60
Mayonnaise	1 Tbsp.	110

Helpful Cooking Hints

A "QUICK" Summary

OF

Herbs & Seeds

DILL
Both leaves and seeds of dill are used. Leaves may be used as a garnish or to cook with fish. Leaves or the whole plant may be used to flavor dill pickles.

FENNEL
Has a sweet hot flavor. Both seeds and leaves are used. Seeds may be used as a spice in very small quantity in pies and baked goods. Leaves may be boiled with fish.

MARJORAM
May be used both green and dry for flavoring soups and ragouts; and in stuffing for all meats and fish.

TARRAGON
Leaves have a hot, pungent taste. Valuable to use in all salads and sauces. Excellent in Tartar sauce. Leaves are pickled with gherkins. Used to flavor vinegar.

CURRY POWDER
A number of spices combined to proper proportions to give a distinct flavor to such dishes as vegetables of all kinds, meat, poultry and fish.

CHIVES
Leaves are used in many ways. May be used in salads, in cream cheese, in sandwiches, omelets, soups, and in fish dishes. Mild flavor of onion.

SAGE
Used fresh and dried. May be used in poultry and meat stuffings; in sausage and practically all meat combinations; in cheese and vegetable combinations, as in vegetable loaf, or curry. The flowers are sometimes used in salads.

continued

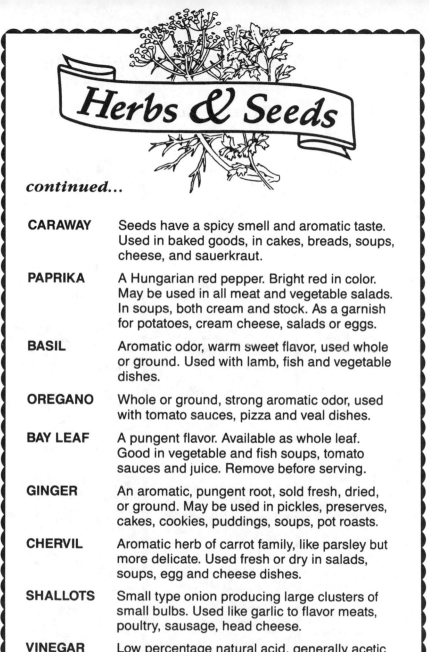

Herbs & Seeds

continued...

CARAWAY   Seeds have a spicy smell and aromatic taste. Used in baked goods, in cakes, breads, soups, cheese, and sauerkraut.

PAPRIKA   A Hungarian red pepper. Bright red in color. May be used in all meat and vegetable salads. In soups, both cream and stock. As a garnish for potatoes, cream cheese, salads or eggs.

BASIL   Aromatic odor, warm sweet flavor, used whole or ground. Used with lamb, fish and vegetable dishes.

OREGANO   Whole or ground, strong aromatic odor, used with tomato sauces, pizza and veal dishes.

BAY LEAF   A pungent flavor. Available as whole leaf. Good in vegetable and fish soups, tomato sauces and juice. Remove before serving.

GINGER   An aromatic, pungent root, sold fresh, dried, or ground. May be used in pickles, preserves, cakes, cookies, puddings, soups, pot roasts.

CHERVIL   Aromatic herb of carrot family, like parsley but more delicate. Used fresh or dry in salads, soups, egg and cheese dishes.

SHALLOTS   Small type onion producing large clusters of small bulbs. Used like garlic to flavor meats, poultry, sausage, head cheese.

VINEGAR   Low percentage natural acid, generally acetic acid. Used as a preservative for all pickling of vegetables and fruit. To give zest or tangy flavor to salad dressings; for meat, fish and vegetable sauces. Different kinds are wine vinegar, malt or beer vinegar, white vinegar, cider vinegar, tarragon vinegar.

RETAIL AND WHOLESALE BEEF CHART

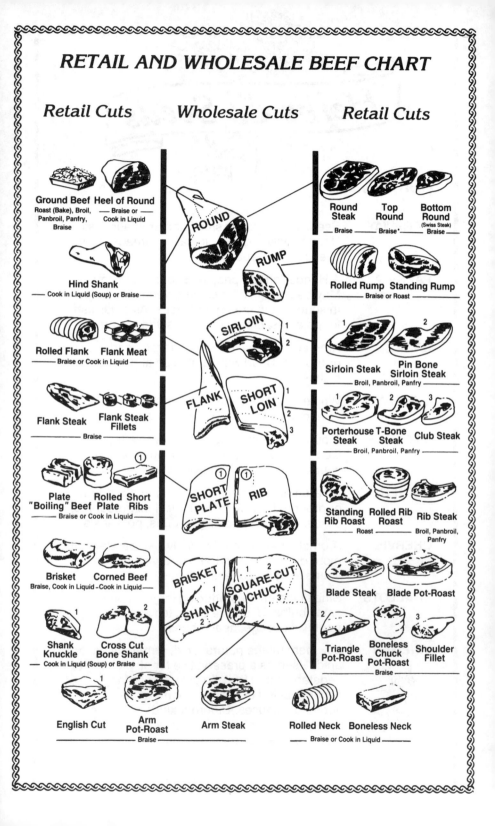

TABLE FOR COOKING VEGETABLES

Vegetable	Ways To Prepare	Cooking	Time
CELERY	Scrub thoroughly. Cut off leaves and trim roots. Slice into desired lengths.	Cook covered in small amount of boiling salted water or in consomme.	10-15 mins.
CORN	Remove husks and silks from fresh corn. Rinse and cook whole.	Cook covered in small amount of boiling salted water; OR cook uncovered in enough boiling salted water to cover ears.	6-8 mins.
EGGPLANT	Wash; If skin is tough, pare. Cut in ½-inch slices.	Dip in beaten egg, then in fine dry bread crumbs. Brown slowly on both sides in hot fat. Season.	Approx. 4 mins.
MUSHROOMS	Wash; cut off tips of stems. Leave whole or slice.	Add to melted butter in skillet; sprinkle with flour and mix. Cover and cook slowly, turning occasionally.	8-10 mins.
OKRA	Wash pods; cut off stems. Slice or leave whole.	Cook covered in small amount of boiling salted water.	8-15 mins.
PARSNIPS	Wash thoroughly; pare or scrape. Slice lengthwise or crosswise.	Cook covered in small amount of boiling salted water.	15-20 mins.
PEAS, Green	Shell and wash.	Cook covered in small amount of boiling salted water.	8-15 mins.
SPINACH	Cut off roots and wash several times in lukewarm water, lifting out of water as you wash.	Cook covered without adding water. Reduce heat when steam forms. Turn often while cooking.	3-5 mins.
TOMATOES	Wash ripened tomatoes.	Cook slowly, covered without adding water.	10-15 mins.
ZUCCHINI	Wash; do not pare. Slice thin.	Season and cook covered in butter in skillet for 5 mins. Uncover and cook till tender, turning slices.	10 mins. Total

Helpful Cooking Hints

QUANTITY COOKING

Food	25 Servings	100 Servings

MEAT, POULTRY OR FISH

Beef and veal (roasted)	10 lbs.	40 lbs.
Fish, large whole	13 lbs.	50 lbs.
Fish, fillets or steaks	7½ lbs.	30 lbs.
Ham (roasted)	10 lbs.	30 lbs.
Hamburger	9 lbs.	35 lbs.
Meat Loaf	5 lbs.	18 lbs.
Pork Rib Roast	10 lbs.	36 lbs.
Pork Chops and Veal Cutlets	9 lbs.	30 lbs.
Turkey or Chicken (roasted)	16 lbs.	50 to 75 lbs.

SANDWICHES

Bread	50 slices	200 slices
Butter	½ lb.	1½ lbs.
Mayonnaise	1 cup	4 to 6 cups
Mixed Filling (meats, eggs, fish)	1½ qts.	5 to 6 qts.
Lettuce	1½ heads	5 to 6 heads

SALADS, CASSEROLES

Potato Salad	4¼ qts.	4½ gals.
Scalloped Potatoes	4½ qts.	17 qts.
Spaghetti	1¼ gals.	5 gals.
Baked Beans	¾ gals.	2½ gals.
Jello Salad	2 qts.	2½ gals.
Lettuce (large heads)	4 heads	12 heads

VEGETABLES

Beets (fresh)	5 lbs.	20 lbs.
Beets (canned)	1 No. 10	4 No. 10
Cabbage (shredded)	5 lbs.	20 lbs.
Carrots (cooked)	6 lbs.	24 lbs.
Corn (canned)	3 No. 2	2 No. 10
Corn (frozen)	3 40-oz. pkgs.	10 40-oz. pkgs.
Peas (fresh)	18 lbs.	70 lbs.
Peas (frozen)	3 40-oz. pkgs.	10 40-oz. pkgs.
Sweet Potatoes (canned)	1 No. 10	4 No. 10
Sweet Potatoes (fresh)	7 lbs.	24 lbs.

Helpful Cooking Hints

Take Time For 10 Things

1. **Take time to work - - -**
   It is the price of success.
2. **Take time to think - - -**
   It is the source of power.
3. **Take time to play - - -**
   It is the secret of youth.
4. **Take time to read - - -**
   It is the foundation of knowledge.
5. **Take time to worship - - -**
   *It is the highway of reverence and washes
   the dust of earth from our eyes.*
6. **Take time to help and enjoy friends - - -**
   It is the source of happiness.
7. **Take time to love - - -**
   It is the one sacrament of life.
8. **Take time to dream - - -**
   It hitches the soul to the stars.
9. **Take time to laugh - - -**
   It is the singing that helps with life's loads.
10. **Take time to plan - - -**
    *It is the secret of being able to have time
    to take time for the first nine things.*

Appetizers, Relishes & Pickles

Soups, Salads & Sauces

Meats & Main Dishes

Vegetables

Breads, Rolls & Pastries

Cakes, Cookies & Desserts

Beverages, Microwave & Misc.

Here's How To Use Your Thumb Index: Place thumb on black tab of the item you want to find. Flip through until a black tab appears under your thumb.